Model Railroad Scratchbuilding

No. 1217
$16.95

Model Railroad Scratchbuilding

by Wayne E. & Mary Cay Wesolowski

 TAB BOOKS Inc.
BLUE RIDGE SUMMIT, PA. 17214

FIRST EDITION

FIRST PRINTING

FEBRUARY 1981

Library of Congress Cataloging in Publication Data

Wesolowski, Wayne E and Mary Cay
    Model railroad scratchbuilding.

    Includes index.
    1. Railroads—Models.   I. Title.
TF197.W37   625.1'9   80-28367
ISBN 0.8306-9657-1
ISBN 0-8306-1217-3 (pbk.)

The locomotive on the cover is clockwork, manufactured by Marklin (in Germany) ca.1900, and is from the collection of Dr. James E. Storer of Lexington, Massachusetts. The photographer was Christian Delbert of Bedford, Massachusetts.

Dedication

To Mary Cay, Tony and Steven

Foreword

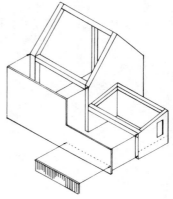

Any meaningful definition of the term "hobby" must include a sense of involvement. Where model railroading is concerned, involvement suggests more than merely setting up a circle of sectional track and running a train around it.

The hobby of model railroading thus truly began, I believe, when someone built a model of something found on or along a real railroad. The date was probably a lot farther back in time than any of us realize. Since today's plethora of kits and parts were not a part of model railroading's formative years, "scratchbuilding"— constructing a model from raw materials—was a necessity rather than an option.

Today, one can choose between model railroads assembled almost exclusively with ready-to-run locomotives and cars which operate amidst structures quickly put together from plastic kits that a child can easily handle; layouts accented with rolling stock and structures largely built up from more difficult "craftsman" kits; or miniature railroads featuring models built from scratch. The art and enjoyment of scratchbuilding is still very much with us, I'm happy to report. It's an option, not a necessity, but it's still alive and well.

Learning to build from scratch isn't hard, and the materials used can be very basic. I think you'll thus enjoy what the author, who is one of the hobby's most creative scratchbuilders, has to say in his *Model Railroad Scratchbuilding*.

J. Anthony Koester, Editor
Railroad Model Craftsman Magazine

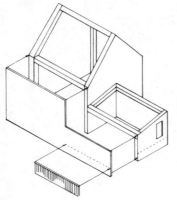

Acknowledgements

Having been a railroad modeler for as long as I can remember, it's very hard, if not impossible, to thank all the people that have had an influence on this book. My mother and father, Dolores and Edward Wesolowski, had a never-ending stream of encouragement and patience while I floundered through the beginning stages of model building. Dad was a lover of model trains and fostered that feeling in me. Through the years, fellow modelers like Frank Pawlikowski, Tim Pawlikowski, Paul Jones, John Kissinger, Lee Gustafson, Larry Easton, Bob Pfister, Bob Walker, Ted Happel and Dave Methlie (Crystal Lake Hobbies) have shared their ideas and good times with me.

The editors at *Railroad Model Craftsman*—in particular Tony Koester who wrote the Foreword and Bill Schaumburg, my former collaborator—have been invaluable aids with drafting, photography and technical problems. Louis Koepel of the Quincy Mining Co., Tom Roberts, John Campbell and Al Henning were valuable in providing information about the Quincy and Torch Lake area structures.

A special thanks to Carstens Publishing Company for allowing us to reprint many of my photographs from previously published articles. I thank Gail Hayes who types most of the manuscript. I am grateful to my mother-in-law, Frances Debowski, who insulated my attic workroom and redecorated my office to encourage the completion of this text.

Finally, my wife, Mary Cay, deserves the most credit for completing this work being combination editor, proofreader, handholder and friend.

Contents

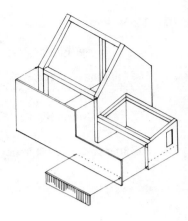

Introduction

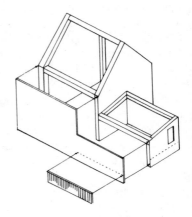

Welcome to the world of model railroad scratchbuilding. The consistent growth of the model railroad hobby can, in part, be attributed to its multifaceted nature. You can not only enjoy the fun of just playing with trains (as I am unabashedly fond of telling my friends), but you also can specialize, or at least dabble, in a wide variety of subjects including things like trackwork, cars, locomotives, prototype operation, scenery, electronics and sound effects, among many others. The list is almost endless. But perhaps one of the most enjoyable aspects of model railroading is making special models for your own pike. One of the great satisfactions of any hobby is the ability to say "I made this." As a beginner you can start with simple kits and then proceed to more advanced or craftsman type kits which will contain possibly hundreds or thousands of parts and castings. One or two steps beyond this type of fun is scratchbuilding, where you not only assemble the model but design it from—and to some degree reproduce—the prototype. The satisfaction now is to say "I created this"—a one of a kind model specifically made for *your* railroad from *your* special set of preferences and values.

For the most part, scratchbuilding is quite inexpensive. Whereas many craftsman kits range upwards from $50 to well over $100, the typical scratchbuilding project even in the larger scales seldom exceeds $10-20. This is because it uses simple materials and your imagination.

The purpose of this book is to introduce you to the tools, methods and thinking of the scratchbuilder. We will be working with some very basic materials like wood, cardstock, and casting plaster. All along, the purpose is to help you create your own models in any scale or railroad motif with a realistic degree of accuracy. To this end I have included a number of projects ranging from relatively simple to quite complex. The simplest have a set of kit-like instructions for you to follow. Try, however, to develop your own construction sequences and modeling methods, even at the very beginning. Notice that up until now I haven't even mentioned scale or gauge. Frequently there is conflict, or at least an elevated sense of competition, between those in O scale, HO scale or N scale or between the narrow gaugers and the standard gaugers. Scratchbuilding transcends these differences, as the techniques are common to *all* scales. Scratchbuilding is fun and your scale preference is really irrelevant.

Although scratchbuilders are active in creating everything from switchstands to locomotives, I believe most begin with structures. Buildings are ubiquitous features of the model landscape and are easy to construct. Electrical work and flawless precision in moving parts are not required. I have, therefore, restricted most of our projects in this book to bridges, buildings, and general railroad structures, along with a healthy dose of information on construction techniques that could be used on any scratchbuilding project.

Well, enough of this talking . . . I think the conductor is swinging his red lantern and shouting a hearty "board" so let's begin our journey into model railroad scratchbuilding.

Wayne E. and Mary Cay Wesolowski

Getting Started

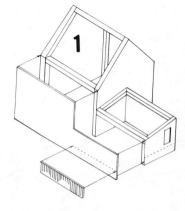

Creating is fun. Whether it's art, music, dance, cooking, or just doing our job most humans find great satisfaction in combining their own talents with personal experience to create something new, different and unique. And it's that spirit of creation which makes scratchbuilding enjoyable. Most anyone can go out and buy a shake-together kit and receive a minimum of satisfaction for his efforts. But there are probably 10,000 other modelers who have the same kit and the same satisfaction. Starting from plans or photographs and building a model from scratch adds an entirely new dimension—your creative spirit. You decide what to include and leave out. You determine scale, color, proportion and material. You are creating a bit of reality. I've always had a special feeling when returning to see a razed prototype, knowing that somehow a little of the spirit and essence of that real structure is saved in my model. Perhaps that's going a little too far, but the one thing this book cannot teach is the desire to create better and better models. If you have it, your skills will grow; if not, enjoy the hobby for what it is and what you can get from it. We should judge ourselves by the satisfaction the hobby gives us, not by another's standards. One man's sloppy model may bring more satisfaction than another's near perfect one. If, however, your enjoyment also comes from a continuing effort to improve, then read on since we have something in common. The desire to create leads one to spend more and more time in developing skills needed to do a better job. Those improved skills will in turn lead to more experience and higher quality workmanship.

SOME THOUGHTS ON SCRATCHBUILDING

Assuming the desire is there, one skill that must be developed to the fullest is the power of observation. We may spend hours at the bench creating a model, but it will only be as good as our ability to reproduce in miniature what we have observed in the prototype. Study a prize winning model at the next model meet you go to. Why did it win? What is there that makes it special? In many cases it is the myriad of fine detail, the little things that, added together, result in a special perfection (Fig. 1-1).

Fig. 1-1. A finely crafted model of a watchman's shanty can be studied for the many details that make it a special model. Notice the very fine window muntins or crosspieces. The stairs are crisp and light. Even the bolts on the wooden piers have been included (Model by Wayne Wesolowski and William Schaumburg).

At some point in the construction process you must decide what is the limit of detail, where to draw the line. When viewing the prototype you must not only observe the shape and form but be able to detach yourself from the scene and zero in on detail and specifics. What are the color tones? How do the corner boards join? What is the purpose of the metal braces? What is the texture of the surface? What seemingly superfluous items capture the feeling of the prototype? All of these added together make the composite that is your model.

PHOTOGRAPHY—A USEFUL TOOL

A good camera can be an invaluable aid to improved scratch-building. My favorite prototype is the Quincy and Torch Lake RR in Upper Peninsula, Michigan, almost 800 miles from my home. Although the Mining Museum is still very active and many cars and locomotives are on display, it is of little value in mid-December back in Illinois when I'm trying to model the back of a building. With the proper photographs I do not need to guess. Several full-view shots taken perpendicular to each side of a building and as many detail photographs as possible are the basis for most complete scratchbuilding projects (Fig. 1-2 through 1-5). For the beginner it might be advantageous to work from plans and/or photos found in the hobby magazines or books rather than begin with a complete scratchbuilding project. I suggest one of the good 35mm SLR (single lens reflex) cameras for the basic picture work. They are light, portable, reasonably priced, and can be used for family and vacation photography as well. It is not unusual for me to take 100 or more photos of a given structure or car—over, under, and around. Before you collapse, the cost of this photographic orgy is not really very high if you only have the film developed and a contact picture sheet made for each roll. The processor will place the small 35mm negatives directly on a sheet of print paper to produce a series of small prints on one 8 x 10 sheet (Fig. 1-6). The price of the contact sheet is a very small fraction of the cost of having all the pictures enlarged and printed in the normal fashion. You can now study (if necessary, with a magnifying glass) many photos at the same time without having to hunt through stacks of prints. Choose for enlargement only those that will be most helpful to you in building your model. The small contact sheet also simplifies the filing and storage of your photographs if the project is not to be done at once. The finished prints give you a second opportunity to practice that skill of observation—but at your leisure (Figs. 1-7, 1-8). I like to settle down by the television or radio with the ball game on and just browse through the enlarged prototype prints. How do these boards join? What is that vent there? How will I model this section? What's the best material, best construction method? It can be a very relaxing and invigorating mental exercise in creation.

For those who are a little deeper into photography, developing and printing your own pictures can bring the cost down to only a few dollars per roll.

Almost all of my photography is done in simple black and white. I use Kodak Plus-X (ASA 125) film that I can develop and print myself, but special skills are not necessary as any camera shop will develop the film and make a contact sheet for you at a nominal cost. Of course, if you do it yourself the cost of the film is the only major expenditure. If you would like to practice darkroom skills without the major investment in equipment, many larger cities have rental photo darkrooms that will provide assistance and supplies besides the actual use of the darkroom.

A few color slides are useful for models that have unusual color schemes. Slides can also be used to make rough scale

Fig. 1-2. Although a real challenge this ponderous building in Hancock, Michigan would be an easy first place model. The variety of construction materials, the montage of wood patterns, the little balcony, false walls, and variety of window styles all add to the model flavor.

Fig. 1-3. A perpendicular view keeps all the construction details in proper perspective. With some basic measurements, such as the total width, or width of a window or door, a simple construction plan could be developed.

drawings by taping a piece of paper to the wall, projecting the slide image on the paper, moving the projector back and forth until the appropriate size image is focused, and finally tracing the structure on the paper.

All the details of both prototype and model photography are beyond the scope of this book. (See TAB book No. 1065 *Model Railroad Photography*). Whether you use a Brownie box camera or the most expensive import the critical directive is to take all the pictures you can of your favorite prototype—today! Nothing will replace the pictures you safely have tucked in your future projects file. And nothing is more disheartening than to see a bulldozer prowling over the remains of a favorite building that you've seen almost every day but just never got around to photographing.

The camera is also a merciless critic of your finished model. Model photography is somewhat more difficult for the beginner, but the ability to observe your finished model perhaps two or three times its size will point out problems and errors we seldom see. The little glue spots and cracks between boards suddenly become huge globs and yawning chasms in the camera's eye (Fig. 1-9).

RESEARCH AND PLANNING

We should not be afraid of criticism, but rather should seek it. Close-up photographs, model contests, and opinions of other modelers are all ways of *improving* our skills and building better models; they should be used as such. Don't leave out a little study as well. *Railroad Model Craftsman* and *Model Railroader* are monthly magazines that provide a regular diet of projects, material reviews, sources of new items, and information on hobby shops and mail order suppliers. Study *all* the articles, even those that don't relate to your latest project. Sometimes there are dandy little hints or construction kinks that will be very helpful. These magazines are designed for you with articles written by regular modelers for other modelers.

We are very fortunate that in the hobby of model railroading almost all of the published material is still available for reading at public and university libraries. Browse through back issues of

Fig. 1-4. The rear of our building offers more details, including a chimney and dormer. Being set in the side of a hill also adds to the modeling character.

Fig. 1-5. Close-ups of all the details are essential. Notice how the foundation is covered with planking only partway along the wall. Take many, many pictures of all the detail—doors, windows, trim, foundations, etc.

Railroad Model Craftsman or *Model Railroader* Magazine and read an article or two by the old masters. I loved Jack Work's articles in the late 1950's, which I consider the golden era of scratchbuilding. Modelers were discovering new materials and pushing back the boundaries of perfection at an accelerating pace. Paul Larson could capture the most intriguing elements of a prototype and recreate it in miniature. Going back even further, modelers like Mel Thornburgh, with only a hand cranked drill, a few files and a soldering iron, created magnificent locomotives and rolling stock that would do modern modelers proud. John Allen's talent ranged from accurate scratchbuilding with micro details to the full fun of operating a model railroad in a true-to-prototype fashion. Modern modelers like Gordon Cannon, Bob Brown, Gene Deimling, and Charles Brummer have adapted new materials and techniques unknown to their earlier colleagues to create fantastic models. Many special interest magazines like the *Narrow Gauge and Shortline Gazette* are filled with very useful articles for the scratchbuilder. Beyond the periodicals are a number of modeling books, many of which are reprints of the old articles mentioned above.

Don't overlook the prototype as a source of information as well. We are trying to recreate the originals, so why not study their methods directly? A number of manuals were published to help railroad shop people keep abreast of the latest methods and

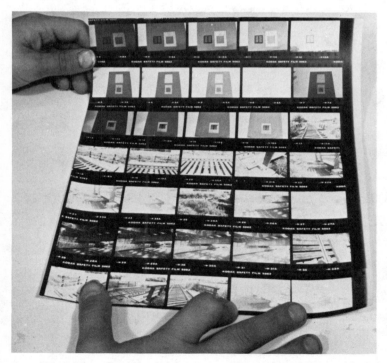

Fig. 1-6. A contact sheet shows how many small pictures can be printed on a single sheet. The compact size and low cost make a contact sheet the ideal way to treat the many detailed photos needed for a good scratchbuilt model.

Fig. 1-7. Jenny's House in Rockford, Illinois simply overflows with detail. The chimneys, round porches and multiple scrollwork ornaments would be a real challenge to a scratchbuilder. I've not yet found the courage to attempt this complex structure, but my photo file has several hundred pictures of every detail.

materials. Many of these are available in whole or part in the Newton Gregg *Train Shed Cyclopedia* series. The drawings and pictures are worth the price alone. Don't get too carried away with prototype construction. For example, modeling interiors may be unnecessary, or laminations may be built easier than board by board construction. Many large university engineering libraries will have back issues of *Railway Age* and *Railway Age Gazette*— prototype trade magazines. Besides the direct technical information about car, locomotive and building construction, they provide a very valuable insight to the feeling, thinking and spirit of the times. If you're modeling the late 1920's, as I do, it's very instructive to read a few issues in that period and see how railroad men thought; what they considered news; what they predicted the future would hold. If you plan to enter model contests, a Xerox of a prototype article can go a long way in supporting your use of a "left-handed digbark" to a skeptical judge. I once found an article about a railroad in California that used special steam jets to blow hordes of migrating caterpillars from the rails since squashed insects make an incredible lubricant that actually kept trains from climbing grades. I've never had the nerve to include those pipes on a locomotive and try to explain it to a contest judge.

Even if the articles don't deal with a model you would like to build, the techniques and the basic approach may be of great value in a later project. Another excellent source of information and advice is your local hobby shop owner. Although much of his business is based on kits and ready-to-run equipment, most shop owners are ardent and advanced modelers who understand scratchbuilding and carry the basic supplies and materials you will

Fig. 1-8. Built by a lumber baron before the turn of the century, Jenny's House has ornate eaves and window cornices. Some special casting techniques like those in Chapter 9 would probably be required.

Fig. 1-9. A close-up nearly twice the size of the model helps check every detail. The character of individual boards, and the large hinges are all clearly shown. Any small errors, gaps or glue marks would be visible. The model is a part of the wing of an old-fashioned snow plow.

need. When the customer rush is off, they usually are most willing to chat about scratchbuilding projects. For those of you far from a local hobby shop, mail order shops such as Coronado Scale Models or Walthers Hobby Shop specialize in materials and parts for the scratchbuilder by mail.

Membership in the National Model Railroad Association will bring a monthly magazine with many plans and ideas for modeling. More important is the right to attend divisional (local), regional, and national meetings or conventions that features clinics, displays, layout tours, and contests where you can observe others' skills and test your own. Best of all, I find the fellowship with people having similar interests most enjoyable. Model railroaders are generally very affable people. I remember approaching John Allen (who was *the* model railroader of his time) at a convention with great trepidation. To my surprise, he was most pleasant, chatted for a few minutes, and even invited me to visit his railroad in California. Needless to say, I literally floated back home after that meeting.

In general, use all the resources at your disposal and don't be afraid to seek new ones. You might try TAB book No. 1021 *The Complete Handbook of Model Railroad Operations* for more ideas, or TAB book No. 786 *The Complete Handbook of Model Railroading*.

HINDSIGHT HINTS

You need not inherit rich Uncle Fred's money to begin scratchbuilding. We'll detail the tools needed for working with different types of materials later on, but we only need say that a few basic tools are necessary and they will not cost a fortune. I would distinguish though between *measuring* and *working* tools. I believe a good measurement is a most important aspect of scratchbuilding. So many models fail to be prize winners because modelers took a liberty here or there, usually with scale size. The smaller your scale, the more important measurement becomes. I would suggest purchasing the best scale rule your finances will allow and perhaps a scale caliper or micrometer. A quality tool will give you years of service. Work tools, like a small hammer or pliers, can be of discount house quality since many times we'll be making special modification by grinding them to new shapes and forms. Don't skimp on knives and cutting tools. Always keep them as sharp as possible. Using several blades for a single model or even a single work session is required for a clean, sharp product. After only a short time, hobby knives become dull and tend to mash and rip the stock rather than slice cleanly through it. Sharpen or replace them often. I use two knife handles—one marked with a piece of tape for the sharpest blades to do the finest cuts; the second for crude cuts. When a knife dulls I put a new blade in the tape-marked handle and transfer the old blade to the second handle.

At times I've seen industrial machine shops with literally acres of highest quality machine tools, rooms of cutting tools, exquisite drafting equipment, and scads of meticulous craftsmen. For a while I wished my shop somehow looked like that. But when I thought about it, I realized that craftsmanship is not a function of the kind of machines and space you have, but rather the intensity and determination of the builder. My shops have ranged in size from a small desk in a bedroom to about half an attic that I now claim as my work room. But the fact really is that most of my new room is parts and materials storage and the actual working space is about two square feet on a chest high table that doubles as a model storage area (Fig. 1-10). The working space continues to dwindle during each project until it's down to a few square inches surrounded by subassemblies, discarded tools, scrap pieces of wood, and other miscellania. At that point a general cleaning is declared and the work starts again in the newly cleared space. Probably the moral of the story is to establish where your work will be done and don't worry about the size.

Lighting is an important aspect of the modeling process. A model built under bright light will look even better under normal light. Shadows on the work have a tendency to distort dimensions, hide detail, and fail to give a clear picture of the model. Two or three lamps with shades are needed to cut out all shadows. At least one should be on a flexible shaft for adjustment without disturbing the modeling work. I have a lamp with a magnifying lens, but seldom use it because the magnified image is not normal for me. Perhaps it is my eyesight—I'm naturally near-sighted, so the magnification doesn't help me a great deal. Perhaps with practice it might be more useful. *Caution:* painting and weathering should be done under the same kind of lighting as the final model will experience. There can be a significant difference in the color of a model under incandescent, fluorescent, and natural light. Fluorescent tends to bring out the blues and greens, while incandescent the reds and oranges. Many modelers have built that "perfect model" at the work bench under ordinary light bulbs only to have it look "strange" when placed on the layout under fluorescents.

Many times I just go stale on a project and need to put it aside for a while. Since there may be many small parts, subassemblies, and other stuff that will stray from the project, I use a set of small shelf-like trays to store each project until finished (Fig. 1-11). These were salvaged from an old store display but any kind of small tray—even cafeteria trays—will do. I keep three to five projects going at the same time. You do tire and need a chance to clear your mind, get some fresh ideas and, in the meantime, mosey to a different project. The trays will keep things in order until you return. One of my favorite projects has been in the works for nine full years, yet when finished, will be one of my best. So don't worry if you procrastinate a little. One of the most valuable sources of material is your own scrap bin. Sometimes entire models are built from the castoffs of other projects. From the beginning, of course, you have no scrap but start saving right now. My mother-in-law saves old toothpaste tubes for the soft metal. My mother is assigned oatmeal boxes. Plastic scrap and little bits of wood are always around. I maintain three scrap boxes—wood, metal, and plastic.

I don't feel there is one particular material that is best for all scratchbuilding projects. Wood, paper, and plastic remain the big three, but which you use or in what combinations are a matter of choice. Begin with one, develop some skill and confidence, then branch off into the others. The broader your base of construction methods and materials, the better your model will be in the long run.

Fig. 1-10. No matter how expensive or elaborate the workbench may be, the actual working space is usually only a few square feet. This workbench is part of an old kitchen cabinet set. Especially cleaned for this photo, bench is never this clean during a construction project.

Fig. 1-11. The shelf-like trays were salvaged from an old store display for spools of thread. Each project is given a tray so small parts, subassemblies, etc., do not wander if the job is set aside for a few days.

Another aspect I feel very strongly about is the idea of prestaining or coloring all materials *before* gluing them together. We do not generally have scale size painters to paint adjacent boards different colors. It's just impossible to keep the different colors from spreading from one board to another. Even if the color is the same you still want some variation from board to board as found in nature. The easiest way is to prestain or color all your stock slightly different colors before gluing. This will also prevent unsightly glue spots from showing up as white or unpainted spots on the finished project. I am also a firm believer in the use of heavy and sometimes *massive* weights and clamps to hold glued objects together while the glue sets. A little patience and a lot of weight will make for a very firm, solid, and crisp joint. A glued joint should have a minimum of glue and a maximum of good smooth contact between surfaces for maximum adhesion. A huge glob of glue just does not hold things together. I have a wide collection of metal bar cut-offs, clamps, clothespins, rubber bands, and other devices to use in holding pieces together. We too often fool ourselves into believing "the glue will hold" only to find an open seam sometime later. You have the choice of taking this chance or clamping, locking, and giving your adhesive an honest opportunity to work. Don't take the chance. Your eye should be the final critic of all construction decisions. We are generally more sensitive to design pattern symmetry and position than to the absolute precision of a measurement. You can tell in an instant if a board is crooked or out of proportion to other pieces in a set but will never notice if they all

27

are a thousandth or two out of scale. It will do you no real good to prove to any observer that a board is exactly the right size if he still feels at first sight that something is wrong. If it's in scale and looks good, then you will have an excellent model. Train your eye and follow it.

SCALE AND GAUGE

All models are built to a predetermined scale or reduced proportion of the original. This book is really designed for *all* modelers without regard to their particular scale, but it might be good to review the various modeling choices so they may be related to the tools and techniques discussed later.

The scales or proportions range from O scale (the largest) to Z scale (the smallest). O scale was once the predominant modeling scale at ¼"-1'O. (That is, each quarter inch of model is equal to one actual foot of prototype.) For example a 40 foot prototype would be 10 inches long when reduced to O scale. The proportion or reduction in size is 1 to 48—an O scale model is exactly 1/48 the size of the original. O scale is the largest of the popular modeling scales and offers the ability to create highly-detailed, actually massive models. Because of their size and weight, O scale cars usually track well and have a prototype feel about them. There *are* disadvantages, especially from a size standpoint. O scale layouts require large amounts of space and usually need large capital investments for cars and locomotives.

The most popular scale is HO at 3.5mm = 1'0". This is roughly Half O scale (thus HO) and is a metric-based system. The proportion or reduction is 1 to 87—that is, an HO scale model is roughly 1/87 the size of the original. Based on its popularity, HO combines the assets of the larger scale in offering good detailing possibility with smaller space requirements. An endless variety of commercial products are available to the hobbyist which may easily be supplemented with scratchbuilt models.

N scale is the smallest popular scale at 1.9mm-1'0" with a proportion of 1 to 160. Its small size makes for a lot of railroad in a very small space. There is a growing cadre of N scale scratch-builders who have done amazing things in this lilliputian scale.

In addition to the scales mentioned, there are a number of other modeling options both larger and smaller so everyone can find his niche. Table I-1 and 1-2 list the major scales, proportions and conversions.

A final word about gauge. The word *gauge* is frequently interchanged with scale as in "O gauge" or "HO gauge." In reality, gauge refers to the spacing between the rails on the railroad track. The standard spacing or *standard gauge* is 4'8½". In normal usage, "HO gauge" would mean the actual dimension (438½') had been reduced to HO scale (about 16.5mm). In this context there is no problem. However, a few railroads had track spacings that were wider or, in most cases, narrower. The best examples are the mining and logging railroads of Colorado, Michigan and Pennsylvania. In many cases, the tracks were spaced at 3'0" to make construction faster and less expensive as well as employ less massive equipment. To call this "HO gauge" would introduce ambiguity, so additional nomenclature has been developed. Modeling, for example, the East Broad Top RR (3'0" between rails) in HO scale would be described as HOn3; meaning HO scale (1/87) on a track spacing of 3 feet. 0n2 would mean modeling all features of the prototype in O scale (1/48) with a track spacing of 2 feet. Many of the more unusual and interesting prototypes used the nonstandard track spacing, and have attracted numerous modelers.

To recap, *scale* means the proportion to which the model is built, while *gauge* refers to the spacing between the rails. Only in the most general cases of colloquial use are scale and gauge interchangeable. As long as you are aware of the difference there is no serious problem.

PLANS

Let's look at plans and drawings for a moment. There is simply no exception but that the best plans are those used by a prototype builder to make the original structure. These are usually quite large (¼" = 1' 0" or larger for details), with probably more information than you might need. However, a surplus of information is generally better than a paucity. Lacking builder's plans the best source would probably be drawings from model magazines or kit plans, generally in HO or smaller. These may present some

Table 1-1. Model Railroad Scales and Proportions.

NAME OF SCALE	SCALE TO FOOT	PROPORTION	CENTER OF COUPLER ABOVE TOP OF RAIL	TRACK GAUGE
O	¼"	1:48	11/16" (17mm)	1.250" (31.76mm)
S	3/16"	1:64	17/32" (13.5mm)	0.875" (22.23mm)
OO	4mm (0.157")	1:76.2	29/64" (11.5mm)	0.750" (19.00mm)
HO	3.5mm (0.138")	1:87.1	25/64" (9.9mm)	0.650" (16.50mm)
TT	1/10"	1:120	9/32" (7.1mm)	0.471" (11.97mm)
N	1.9mm (0.075")	1:160	0.216" (5.5mm)	0.354" (9.00mm)
Z	1.38mm (0.0544")	1:220		0.256" (6.50mm)

Table 1-2. Model Railroad Scale Conversion Chart. To Convert Any Measurement From the Scale in the Vertical Column to the Scale Along the Top, Multiply by the Figure Shown.

	0	S	00	HO	TT	N	Z
0	1	.750	.630	.551	.400	.300	.218
S	1.333	1	.840	.735	.553	.400	.290
00	1.585	1.190	1	.875	.635	.476	.346
HO	1.815	1.360	1.143	1	.725	.544	.396
TT	2.500	1.875	1.575	1.377	1	.750	.545
N	3.333	2.500	2.100	1.837	1.333	1	.727
Z	4.583	3.437	2.887	2.526	1.833	1.375	1

problems. The plans that appear in magazines are in a pictorial style, drawn by the draftsman in ⅜" scale or larger to include all the detail. They are reduced photographically for esthetic appeal, then printed in the magazine. However, as the size goes down the ability of the modeler to read and transfer a dimension decreases. Look for the largest size plans you can get. Those 0 scale plans are much better since you can read the scale inches more clearly. If possible, have the plans in the magazine copied by a blueprint shop. Get copies *exactly* to your scale for laying out walls and such directly over the plans. (Copies should be large enough to measure the detail accurately.) On many actual construction drawings all the board sizes are written in so no measuring is required.

Two additional problems with the magazine plans are the *French shading* and *printing error*. Examine a drawing in the magazine carefully (even mine in this book) and you'll notice that some of the lines are darker (actually wider) than others. This is called *French shading* and gives the drawings a little body and contrast. At the same time, it is more difficult to locate the end of a dimension, especially if the shading is heavy. Engineering drawings normally have uniform line weights to avoid this problem. Also there is a slight printing error in most magazines that ranges up to 3%. This is not noticeable in small objects or large scale, but as the scale gets smaller the error increases. Look at a drawing of a long passenger car drawn in HO or N. Measure the full length of the car with your scale rule and compare it to the printed dimension usually given under the car. On a 60 foot car you may have an error of as much as 1.5 scale feet. A simple solution to the problem is to have enlargements of plans made indicating the *exact* length of the car or building in your scale—"enlarge this plan so the length of the car is *exactly* 260mm or 5.64 inches." Or seek copies of the original plans. Or just be aware that these kinds of discrepancies *do* exist and be prepared to live with them. In many cases I'm willing to take a little less accurate model than to go through all the special pains to make a perfect one and perhaps lose interest and not have one at all.

COMPONENT PARTS

About ten years ago I remember being at a meeting of the Northern Illinois Society of Model Engineers where Frank Pawlikowski showed me a model window. The detail was beautiful with thin muntins (the little pieces that separate the window panes) and even wood grain in the frames, but they were *plastic castings*. Oh, ugh, how awful . . . imagine a plastic casting of a window. I had always admired Frank's work (especially with locomotives) but how could he stoop so low! At that time I was trying to build windows from 30-40 little pieces of wood and lots of patience.

Fig. 1-12. Commercial castings offer a chance to save a great deal of time in scratchbuilding. Imagine how long it would take to build all the little framing parts in the windows shown at the bottom of the photo. At the top is a freight car air brake cylinder, followed by door frame castings, small bolts and hinges, and finally a collection of windows. Cost is generally around $1.00 for 3-5 castings, depending on complexity.

Frank was right, however. Over the years, I've grown to use almost every kind of component casting possible. For maybe the three windows in a very special contest model, the individual board method might be necessary; but for a good layout model component, castings are indispensable. Low in cost, castings for windows, doors, vents, roof details, fences, railings, nuts, bolts, and so forth are available at your hobby shop from several different manufacturers. They are easy to paint and may be cut apart and reassembled into special forms for your own scratchbuilt models. In no way do I feel this is a compromise with basic scratchbuilding. The enormous amount of time saved can be better used in the creation of many more and interesting models (Fig. 1-12).

That's pretty much an overview of my feelings and thoughts on scratchbuilding. Take the best, forget the worst and let's go on to some detailed projects and ideas about working with wood, paper and plaster.

Basic Tools
And Techniques

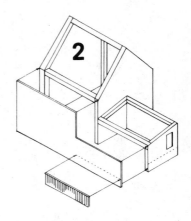

One of the nicer aspects of scratchbuilding is that it is relatively inexpensive and can be successfully started with a minimum of tools. In this section we'll discuss the basic tools necessary and some of the techniques used by scratchbuilders. Remember, though, that my own collection of tools is the result of more than 20 years of scratchbuilding with plenty of trading and scrounging thrown in. By no means are you expected to rush out and buy everything I suggest. I have prepared what I feel is a minimum list of tools in Table 2-1.

Creating models of prototype structures requires a certain amount of discipline. By this I mean that it will be easy to say "Oh, that looks good enough" when you really mean "I don't feel like checking any closer." Try to avoid the temptation to compromise. The more frequently you take the tougher road and build a model as close to scale as possible, the more it will become a personal habit with the associated satisfaction of knowing you have done things correctly. Your most effective weapon in creating accurate models are the various measuring and layout tools.

MEASURING TOOLS

Rulers come in a variety of forms, but are all designed to allow you to make a comparison between your item and a known dimension. Your first tool should be the very best scale rule you can afford. These are usually metal rulers engraved with scale corresponding to the regular model scales—usually HO, O, S, and possibly N. They read directly in scale feet and inches and are your prime source of accuracy. Look for rulers with clear sharp markings that are not likely to wear off. Many have additional scales such as metric or full size feet and inches on the reverse. Since this is your primary way of measuring, and therefore building, your models it *must* be good. Don't fall into the trap of looking for only your scale since many times you will be working with plans in possibly N scale which you must then convert to your own scale—perhaps HO. Just use the scale rule twice . . . take the dimensions off the plan in N then use the same units in HO for your models.

It may be helpful to have a good machinist's ruler reading in 1/64 or, better yet, 1/100 of an inch (Fig. 2-1). These are most useful for modelers in scales that relate directly to the English units $(0; \frac{1}{4}'' = 1'0'', S; 3/16'' = 1'0'')$ where a finely divided metric rule would be better for the metric scales $(HO; 3.5mm = 1'0'', N; 1.9mm = 1'0'')$. I prefer to think almost exclusively in the scale feet and inches. With all the other problems associated with scratchbuilding, there is no sense in adding more work and confusion by making numerous scale conversions. It's useful to have a long steel straightedge for scribing lines and a short one for easy handling in cramped spaces.

In addition to scale rules and machinist's rules, as your skills increase it might be useful to purchase an engineer's and architect's triangular rule (Fig. 2-2). These normally have six different scales

Table 2-1. Suggested Starter's Set of Basic Tools.

2 X-acto Knife Handles
1 Package each #11, #16 X-acto Knife Blades
1 Zona Saw - Fine Tooth
1 Scale Rule - 12" Length
1 Set Small Drills or Select Common Sizes
1 Pin Vise for Drills
1 Package Single-Edged Razor Blades
1 Miter Box
1 Pair Tweezers
1 Set Pattern Files
1 Large File (Mill Face) 6" or Longer
   Assorted Small Pieces Flex-i-Grit
   and Sandpaper
1 Large Bag Spring-Type Clothespins
   Weights
   Number 2 Pencils
1 Scriber (Pin Stuck in Wood Dowel)
1 Square (Inexpensive Combination Type)
1 Small vise

Fig. 2-1. Using two rulers to measure the height of this scale man, it's clear that the machinist's ruler with divisions down to 1/64″ is much more accurate than the crude ruler or yard stick measurements. The better the ruler the better your ability to make a measurement.

per ruler. The architect's rule generally provides scales ranging from 1/16 = 1′0″ to 1½″ = 1′0″, and are very useful for reading large scale plans and blueprints, such as original erection drawings for a railroad car or locomotive. The engineer's rules are generally multi-proportion rules ranging from 10 to 100 units per inch. I use them for selective compression to reduce the proportion of drawings uniformly. Suppose, for example, that the overall length of a building is 65 scale feet. I would measure the plan first and if I wanted to reduce the structure by about ½, I would measure the plan first with the 10 unit scale, then just flip the ruler to the 20 unit scale and mark that distance on the building material. All other dimensions could then be reduced in a similar way (Fig. 2-3). This saves a considerable amount of arithmetic and eliminates many computational errors.

For more exacting work, a scale caliper is very useful (Fig. 2-4). Although they are relatively expensive, if you need to know a dimension down to a scale gnat's eyelash, the caliper is very useful. The caliper is a precision measuring tool engraved with scale feet and inches and is read to the nearest ⅛ of a scale inch. You can really determine if a 2 x 4 is a 2 x 4. In many cases I use the caliper to transfer dimensions directly to the work. It can be used to check spacing and will function as a depth gauge. The exact dimension can be easily set on the caliper and then the work fashioned to fit that dimension. A dial caliper reads the final few thousandths of an inch on a large dial with a moving hand, considerably reducing error in

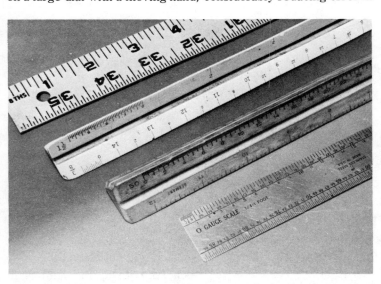

Fig. 2-2. Several different types of rulers used by modelers. At the top is a simple yard stick used for very crude measurements. The second is a triangular architect's rule with six different scale rules in one. Being made from wood or plastic it cannot be employed for a straight edge when cutting. Its major use is for reading or making plans in different scales. The third ruler is an engineer's scale with six different numerical scales also used for reading drawings. The bottom metal ruler is a model railroad scale rule. Scales include O, HO and S, plus metric and ordinary English scales on the reverse side. This is the real workhorse of a modeler's collection and should be of the best quality possible.

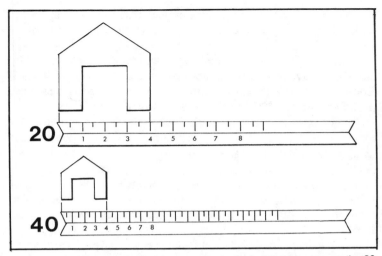

Fig. 2-3. Measure the larger drawing on any scale. In this case, we use the 20 unit scale. Turning to the 40 unit scale automatically reduces the dimension by ½. Had the 60 unit scale been used, the reduction would be ⅓. Enlargement may be made by reversing the procedure.

reading. With a scale conversion table, any caliper can be effectively used in model building. Costs will range from $15 on up to over $100 depending on quality. Scale calipers cost about $30.

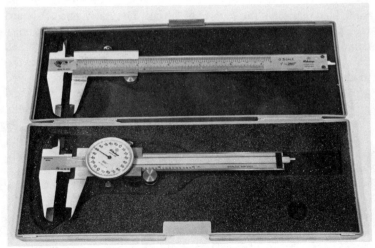

Fig. 2-4. At the top of the case is a scale caliper that reads to ⅛ of an 0 scale inch. For very critical modeling, a caliper is the ultimate tool. The lower caliper has a dial reading in 0.001″ directly.

Dividers are two-legged instruments that are used to transfer dimensions from one plan to the work piece. They resemble a simple compass without the pencil point (Fig. 2-5). If you have drawings already in your scale, the dividers can be used to rapidly and accurately transfer the dimensions without using a scale rule. Because of their very sharp points, they can be used to make small pin holes for reference points on the work piece.

Pencils will quickly dull with use if sharpened to a point. A dot made with a dull pencil will be several scale inches in diameter. If used, pencils should be quite hard (4H) and sharpened to a chisel point on a piece of sandpaper (Fig. 2-6). An alternative is to use a scriber or pinpoint that may be inexpensively made by grinding off the top of a straight pin and forcing it into a dowel handle. The scribed line is sharper and more consistent than a pencil mark (Fig. 2-5).

Since many lines must be drawn exactly square to the edge of a piece of material, it's necessary to have a square of some sort. A typical Sears 6-inch combination square is a good place to start, although I also use a fine 3-inch machinist's square for working with smaller pieces (Fig. 2-7).

CUTTING TOOLS

Cutting wood and plastic for models is not always an easy task. We use tools to cut pine and ordinary building materials without thinking much about the surface of the cut. The rough end of a board that might be perfectly acceptable in *real* house construction is completely out of scale for a model. We need a very smooth and finished surface. The most common type of saw used by the modeler is a Zona or razor saw. It's a "back saw" with a reinforced strip at the top of a thin blade and can usually cut both wood and metal. I like to reserve one tool exclusively for wood. Because of the long grain in basswood, it is very easy to tear and rip the edge. A saw with fewer than 50-70 teeth per inch will result in a very rough and jagged end that will have to be sanded or filed smooth. With a finer blade it is possible to make a relatively smooth cut. Usually some kind of square or miter gauge is used to keep the saw cut straight and true. These are available from commercial sources, but you can make one to your own specifications from several short pieces of wood (Fig. 2-8).

For cutting small wood strips, the choice of many modelers is a razor knife or scalpel—type knife. Simple single-edged razor blades sold in hardware stores are a good tool which may be

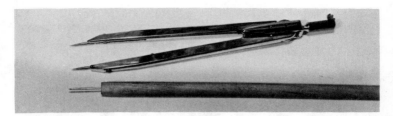

Fig. 2-5. A pair of dividers can be used for transferring dimensions directly from a plan to the model. The lower scriber for marking soft materials is made by forcing a headless pin into a piece of dowel stock.

purchased in bulk packs of up to 100 at very reasonable prices. They have the disadvantage of being relatively large compared to the models, and are therefore a bit difficult to maneuver into some small spaces. A typical modeler's knife is shown in Fig. 2-9. These are sold by X-acto and others with several different handle and holder styles, along with a wide variety of blades. I tend to use just two. The first is a #11, which is a very thin long pointed blade. This is excellent for trimming fine detail in very tight places. The main disadvantage I find is that it is long and may at times over-cut—that is, you cut, press down and cut a little more than you want. More often I use a #16 blade since it has a shorter length but is just as sharp and there is a little better control. The most important factor is to have a very, *very* sharp knife at all times. As the blade dulls, it tends to crush the wood and the knife does not follow a true line but wanders through the wood. This usually results in a slanted rather

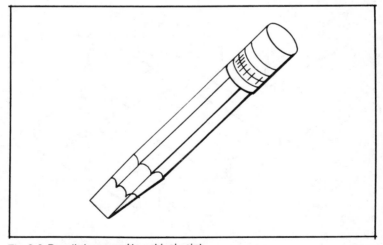

Fig. 2-6. Pencil sharpened to a chisel point.

Fig. 2-7. Squares are essential for keeping models properly aligned. The larger one is for major structures and O scale work. The smaller square is only 3″ long and easily fits into small spaces. Many large stores like Sears have a variety of small squares available.

than a straight cut. Some modelers do resharpen their knives on a small stone but I have yet to be successful at that. Since the blades are relatively inexpensive I find it more economical in terms of my time to just throw the old ones away and use a new knife. I generally keep two knives in use—one with the handle marked with a piece of tape for my freshest and sharpest blade. This is used for the finest detail work. When the blade begins to dull, it is transferred to a second handle and used for the less exacting cutting work.

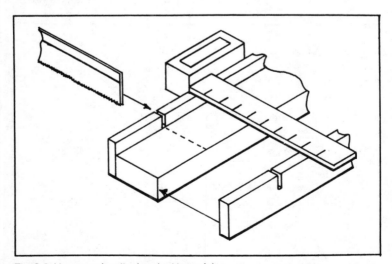

Fig. 2-8. Homemade miter box (not to scale).

40

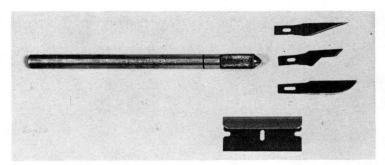

Fig. 2-9. The modeling knife is essential for the modeler. This is an X-acto handle with a #11, #16, and #9 blades (top to bottom). The single-edged razor blade, when purchased in bulk, can also be a very inexpensive cutting tool.

Medical-type scalpels are available from several suppliers, with a convenient and easy-to-hold handle. The disadvantage is that many of the blades are long and curved, thus difficult to get into small places. They may not be legal in some states.

For cutting large circles in thin wood or paper, a compass knife is most effective. Made from a small piece of sharpened steel, it fits directly into the leg of a draftsman's compass in exactly the same fashion as an ordinary piece of pencil lead (Fig. 2-10). Don't skimp; buy the best compass you can afford, since less sturdy models will flex and bend under stress and not cut a true circle. Use only light pressure and make several passes to cut through.

A large wallpaper knife for cutting thick cardboard completes the set of hand cutters.

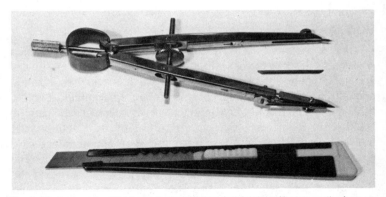

Fig. 2-10. A compass fitted with a steel knife edge (pictured between the legs of the compass) will cut perfect circles in most light materials. An inexpensive wallpaper knife with a renewable blade is very helpful for rough cutting such as cardboard or insulation.

The cutting surface deserves some comment. Although a chef may like a beautiful solid chunk of wood for a chopping block, solid wood makes a poor cutting board. Select a piece of Masonite, pressed board, plastic, or other semi-hard material that does *not* have a grain because wood, plywood, and even paper have a surface grain that the knife will follow instead of the straight edge. The knife will not wander as much on a grain-free surface.

CUTTING MACHINERY

Many times you must cut a large number of pieces to an identical length, which is almost impossible when cutting them individually. I find in these cases it is best to cut them slightly oversized, then clamp the pieces together and sand down the ends at one time to the correct and identical length (Fig. 2-11). If this is too much bother, there are several commercial tools available to ease the job. The "chopper" (Fig. 2-12) is an ordinary single-edged razor mounted in an arm mechanism that "chops down" across the wood piece. A metal stop mechanism allows the length to be cut repetitively. My stop tends to drift a little and I really have to clamp it down tight to prevent slipping. As the razor dulls it will drift considerably, especially in the larger O scale pieces. This will probably not be as much of a problem in the smaller scales.

Razors work best with a slicing action rather than direct pressure, so the Shay wood miter uses a sliding action to cut across the wood. The device works better on the larger pieces, but may require more adjustments to the rather complicated mechanism (Fig. 2-13).

FILES AND SANDPAPER

Files are most useful for finishing metal, plastic, and even wood to a desired texture (Fig. 2-14). If an opening is slightly undersized, a few strokes with a sharp file may easily enlarge the opening. A round file is especially useful for enlarging drill holes. Files come in several different sizes and textures or face cuts. A small set of hobby (needle or pattern) files will easily satisfy most needs. Select those with a sharp point. As a simple substitute, emery boards used for manicuring may be substituted in some circumstances. For special finishing purposes, like sanding the individual siding boards on a structure, a special sanding board may be made by gluing small pieces of sandpaper to a wooden stick of the appropriate size. Special curved files called *riffles* and micro-sized files may be purchased from the Brookstone Company.

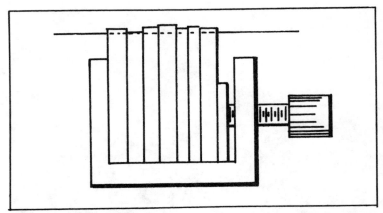

Fig. 2-11. To make a number of parts to identical length, clamp them together and finish with a file.

Finally, one or two large files with mill or bastard faces are useful for rough sanding of very large pieces.

Another way of finishing surfaces is to use sandpaper. Various grades of abrasives are attached either to paper or to a plastic backing. Commercial wet-or-dry 10″ x 12″ sheets available at hardware stores make a good starting point. Flex-i-grit packets

Fig. 2-12. The "chopper" is a commercial product available at most hobby shops that will cut a number of copies of light wood to identical lengths. It is less effective for larger pieces.

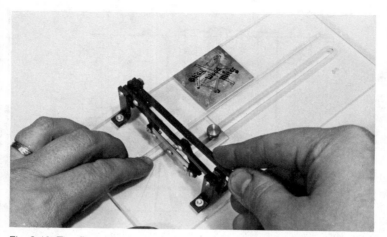

Fig. 2-13. The Shay wood miter uses a slicing action to cut through light wood. More effective for larger pieces the rather complicated mechanism does required adjustment from time to time.

with a Mylar backing have sheets of many different grades and can be bent and flexed to fit almost any contour.

TWEEZERS, CLAMPS, WEIGHTS AND HOLDING DEVICES

Perhaps the most important tool you will purchase is a good set of tweezers. The human hand is just too big to handle many of the pieces of material we will need. Tweezers are a natural extension of the hand. They should feel right; not too heavy and most importantly, not too stiff. Squeezing the tweezers should take almost no effort. If too stiff, squeezing will cause your muscles to quiver every so slightly and your control will seriously diminish. I

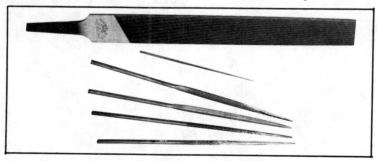

Fig. 2-14. A set of pattern files (bottom) are useful for wood and metal. The micro file (middle) has only occasional use, but when the clearances are very tight there is no substitute. The large file with a mill face is good for removing large quantities of materials, including roughing out projects in wood and plaster.

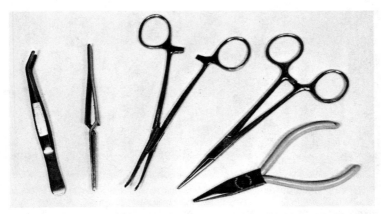

Fig. 2-15. Our fingers are just too big and rough to handle some of the smallest model parts. From left to right: a good set of tweezers with a very soft feel (some modelers like a much sharper point); reverse action or clamping tweezers (these are normally closed and can be used for a very light clamp); two pairs of hemostats—one curved and one straight (with small locks on the handles, they make excellent clamps while painting or handling rather hard objects); a set of small pliers finishes the set of holding tools. Pliers can be ground to different contours for special holding projects.

use a rather blunt serrated head tweezers for almost all my work. Many modelers like very pointed ones.

To complement the tweezers, I use a number of medical clamps called *hemostats*. These are similar to tweezers with handles that may be locked in place with a clamping mechanism on the handle. For holding parts for painting or clamping small pieces, these are very useful. Biology tool sets, frequently available

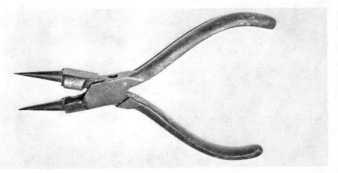

Fig. 2-16. Round nose jeweler's pliers are used to roll wire into perfect circles. This just cannot be done with a regular set of pliers. The cutters also can be used for cutting wire stock.

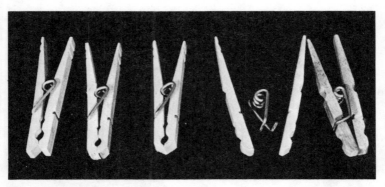

Fig. 2-17. Spring action clothespins are inexpensive clamps. On the left is a regular clothes pin. Note that the faces meet well back from the tip, making them inappropriate for holding small items. The second and third pins have had the tips sanded back to make a better clamping surface. The fourth and fifth show a simple trick to improve the pins without any sanding. Simply take the wooden parts out of the spring mechanism and reverse them back to back. That will at least give a sharper tip.

second-hand at college book stores, are a good source of the smaller tools.

Several small pliers, usually a flat needle-nose type, are handy. I especially recommend a set of round-nose jeweler's pliers for bending wire into eyelets, chain links and curved sections. It's almost impossible to get a pure round curvature without those special pliers (Figs. 2-15, 2-16).

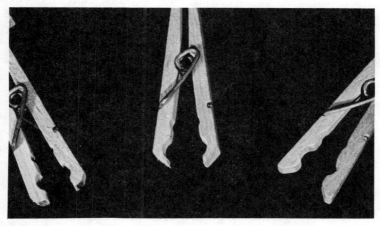

Fig. 2-18. Close up of the tips of several wooden clothespins show how a little grinding or sanding can improve the pincer power compared to the regular clamp at the right.

46

Fig. 2-19. Don't be afraid to use as many pins as necessary to firmly clamp a section in place while the glue dries.

I am a very strong advocate of lots of clamps and plenty of patience while the glue is drying. Any adhesive needs time to set, and the tighter the contact while the joint is fluid, the tighter the finished joint will be. Clothespins and rubber bands are the first and least expensive form of clamps. For a dollar or two you can purchase a bag of 100 spring-type wooden clothespins. At that price, I have no qualms at all about sanding and filing them to any shape needed. A blunt flat face or a sharp pointed face are the most useful. In their normal state, the faces are cut back and don't clamp small objects very well (Figs. 2-17 through 2-19).

I save all the rubber bands from the daily paper for use in modeling work. Use as many as necessary to hold odd or hard-to-clamp objects together. When the glue has set simply cut

Fig. 2-20. Weights should be as heavy as the job calls for. A small metal bolt (left) is fine for small parts but the railroad spike and the large cutoff pieces of metal are great for larger areas.

them away with a razor rather than run the risk of pulling the bands off and possibly damaging the model.

Large flat surfaces also require clamping, but of a different kind. Pressure must be spread and held over a large area. I use

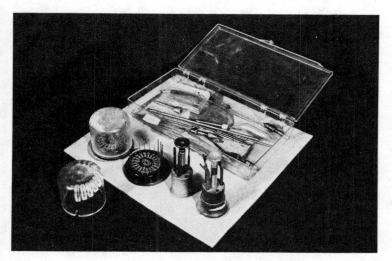

Fig. 2-21. Over the years you collect a lot of small drills and parts. I glued a plastic box, as well as small drill cases, a set of jeweler's screwdrivers, and wrenches to a piece of wood. Not all of this is required for the beginning modeler—perhaps only a few of the wire size drills, depending on your scale, and a pin vice or holder for the drills.

48

Fig. 2-22. A wooden fixture or jig made from short pieces of wood glued and tacked to a wooden base. The wood frame from a large coaling tower is shown in place. When making several copies of the same item, such a fixture is very useful to assure that all will be identical.

scraps and cut-offs from large metal bars purchased at a local machine shop. Weighing up to one pound each, they really hold a part in place. The square ones double as a machinist's square to maintain perpendicularity. It's surprising how strong models really

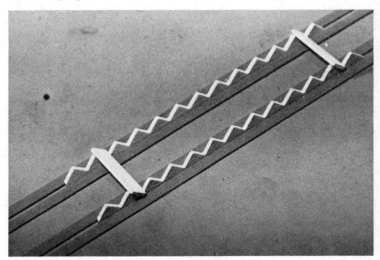

Fig. 2-23. Gluing four pieces of wood to a wood or cardstock base makes a simple fixture for making stairs. The space between the gaps should be equal to the space between the stringers or side boards for the stairs.

are and how tight the joints will be when pressed until dry. For a small fee, many machine shops will supply these end pieces. An old railroad spike makes an interesting weight, since the head has a projection that can be used to concentrate the force at one point. Smaller weights, such as large nuts or fittings, are also valuable for more delicate work (Fig. 2-20). For less stringent holding purposes, simple masking and Scotch tape are very useful. Although the tape will not provide the rock-hard holding power of the weights, it is usable for more temporary work such as holding very small parts in place while spray painting and masking parts. A small modeler's vise completes the set of clamps and holding tools.

DRILLS

A set of drills from ¼" to 1/16" graduated in 64ths is the largest type a modeler will ever need. The "wire sizes" or small drills from No. 60 to No. 80 are used more frequently by modelers and can be purchased in sets or individually. I have one complete set but find that I use mainly a few. These, of course, are the ones that most often break and need replacement. Pin vises may be used to hold the drills for hand boring. A smaller reamer or tapered round minifile may be used to expand the size of a hole, thus further limiting the need for many drills (Fig. 2-21).

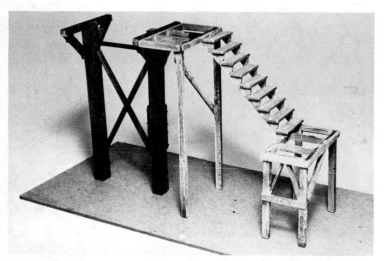

Fig. 2-24. The risers or step portion of the stairs are glued in place. Glue one at the top and bottom first to rigidize the set. Add the rest as desired.

Fig. 2-25. The finished stairs on the shanty are light and dainty but add a special character to the model which would be rather plain without it.

FIXTURES AND FRAMES

Whenever more than three identical copies of a piece must be made, I will use a fixture (sometimes called a *jig*) to hold the basic parts in exactly the same location for each piece (Fig. 2-22). There is always a great temptation to just make a few, but experience will teach you that, done freehand, no two pieces will be identical. The fixtures need not be elaborate; just a wood or cardboard base and a few strips of wood to hold things in place. A very simple example is a fixture to hold the stringers for a stairway (Fig. 2-23). When putting all the little steps (risers), in place, the two side beams (stringers) must be parallel and steady until the glue sets. By gluing four pieces of wood to a base (each pair to hold one of the stringers), the stairs can be efficiently and accurately formed. Glue the top and bottom steps on first. That will fix the spacing between the risers as other steps are added. The stairs in the elevated shanty (Figs. 2-24, 2-25) were made on just such a fixture.

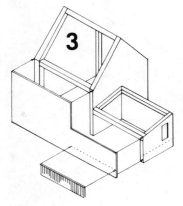

Working With Wood

Wood is a marvelous building and modeling material that has been a favorite of mankind for centuries. Miniature wooden boats have been found in the tombs of Egyptian Pharoahs, proving that model building in wood is an activity which is several thousand years old. It's a medium easy to cut and carve; it glues with a wide variety of adhesives; it will readily take many different types of finishes; and it is really quite inexpensive.

Used for construction of man's homes and shelters from the beginning of construction techniques, wood may be easily worked with power tools as well as hand instruments.

Railroads frequently are forced to construct buildings from local materials to local specifications which means "build it with whatever you got." Many small wooden structures abound at railside, including storage buildings, handcar sheds, coaling towers, crew quarters, office buildings, and even foundries and roundhouses. The older and more rural the railroad, the more likely that wooden structures predominate. Perhaps one of the most spectacular uses of wood is the huge yet delicate trestles and bridges which span many chasms. Frequently, millions of board feet of timber were harvested from local forests to create giant trestles, some hundreds of feet high. Next time you travel on a highway paralleling a rail route, count the number of small trestles and culverts. Depending on topography, one or more per mile is not uncommon.

Today there are new modeling media that are attempting to simulate wood. Several model kit companies make one—piece structure models in high—density urethane and polyester plastics. Some even use plaster to simulate wood. These can be highly effective *if* (and it's a big if) the modeler is capable of painting and finishing the plaster or plastic to look like wood. It is not always an easy task. Wood does its best at simulating wood and any modeler can easily create masterful looking wooden models (Figs. 3-1 though 3-4). A number of model suppliers have wood products specifically designed for the model railroader. With stains and paints it's easy to simulate aged, weathered or new, freshly painted wood. Many modelers are experienced in working with wood from repairing the house or building something for the kids, so it is a natural starting point for model work. In small structures, it is also possible to use prototype construction practice with almost board-by-board construction. This is the way to prize-winning models. Take a look at a first place wooden model. In most cases, one of the most striking yet subtle features is the individual grain and weathering of separate boards.

Examine an old or aging prototype structure. Notice how different boards weather and age at different rates. Some have extra coarse grain and knotholes while others are smooth. This can easily be simulated by building up your structures from boards that are prestained varying colors and scrambled before construction. More on this later.

Fig. 3-1. This old-time snow plow called a "snow crab" was built almost entirely from pieces of scale lumber prestained a weathered gray. The variation of the boards can easily be seen on the plow blades. Pieces of plaster were used to simulate the concrete counterweights in the car.

Fig. 3-2. This fine old water tower is made by gluing many pieces of stripwood onto an ordinary oat meal box. The foundation piers are cast from plaster. All the boards are pre-stained before attaching to the model.

TYPES OF WOOD

Although there are literally dozens of different kinds of timber used in manufacturing, ranging from apple wood to zebra wood, the modeling hobby has basically limited itself to three types—balsa, basswood, and pine.

Balsa wood is very light, open-grained wood that has frequent use in the model airplane hobby because of its lightness. It is difficult to cut, easily crushes under the pressure of the knife, and

Fig. 3-3. A century-old freighthouse in Lombard, Illinois along the Chicago and Northwestern RR was the prototype for this wooden model. Again, separate boards were ganged together for the siding and the character of the individual boards is evident. The foundations and chimney are plaster, while the roof is cardstock covered with masking tape and weathered with chalk dust. The windows and doors are Grandt Line plastic castings, while the stairs are built up from small pieces of scale lumber.

Fig. 3-4. The Quincy Mining Company in Michigan's Upper Peninsula created entire towns for their workers at the turn of the century. This model of a miner's house is from Lower Pewaubic, Michigan—a town that is mostly foundations and weeds today. Construction is large pieces of sheetwood (clapboard surface) with plastic window and door castings. The foundation is solid plaster with small stones embedded throughout the mix.

has an insatiable thirst for paint and stains. It is *not* a major wood for the serious model railroader.

Clear pine is frequently used by kit manufacturers for large blocks such as the ends and bases of house or boxcar kits. It is more dense and harder than basswood and cuts easily with a power saw, but is difficult to cut with modeling tools. Availability is good at better lumber yards, but it is generally not used by the novice modeler.

Basswood is the lightest of the hardwoods and is virtually the sole wood used by the major kit and material manufacturers. Because it is so light, basswood is more difficult to carve than cherry or walnut and tends to split rather easily along its grain. Perhaps its most annoying quality is an unpleasant fuzz or surface grain that leaps up upon the application of paint or stain. In addition, large pieces cut on a power saw will easily burn if the blade is not razor sharp.

Despite these difficulties, basswood is the best available modeling wood. It is hard enough to hold its shape and provide sufficient strength for the model while exhibiting a fine grain and good paint-holding characteristics. It's also soft enough to cut with most modeling tools. As we go along I will point out ways to simplify your use of basswood and to overcome its shortcomings.

WOOD STOCK

Wood for the modeler comes in a variety of formats. The most crude are basswood blocks and sheets from cabinetmakers' supply shops. These are quite large—usually several inches square for "turning blocks" and sheets ranging from ⅛″ x 5″ on up to regular 2x4's. The price per foot or pound of wood is quite low, but you have a lot of work to do in order to be able to use it. Many modelers, especially those working in the larger scales, will start with this stock and cut smaller pieces on a power saw. These techniques are beyond the scope of this book, but as you develop your skills and your need for very large quantities of cut wood increases it might be an area to investigate.

Stripwood

Many manufacturers cut basswood down to certain common fractional sizes such as ⅛″x1/16″ or ¼x3/32″. These are generally called *stripwood* and usually sold in lengths up to 24″ that are not related to any particular scale or gauge.

Scale Lumber

Several manufacturers have commercially available basswood machined to scale lumber sizes; that is, actual 2"x4"s or 2"x12"s correctly dimensioned for your scale (Fig. 3-5). Currently this type of material is available only for modelers in HO and O scale. These are rough-sized lumber pieces, *not* finished lumber, so a 2x4 is actually 2 scale inches by 4 scale inches while a piece of lumber you buy in the lumber yard is not a 2x4 but is actually finished down just slightly to about 1¾"x3¾". In all but the largest scales and most exacting models this will make little difference. However, there are no rules that you must only use O scale lumber if you model in O scale. I frequently jump between HO, O and stripwood sizes to find the piece of lumber that is most suited to the work I am doing at the moment. For example, the little cross pieces in a window (called muntins) are about ¾"x½". While no O scale piece is available, an HO 1x2 easily fits the bill. To help you in selecting the correct lumber size for the job, I've developed simple conversion tables for all the currently available lumber and stripwood sizes (Tables 3-1 through 3-3).

Structural and Specialty Shapes

In addition to the lumber and stripwood selection, there are also available a number of different structural shapes and forms in wood. These include items like H-columns, I-beams, Z-braces, dowels, quarter round, door track, channels, and numerous other items. Properly finished, they can simulate metal for those who

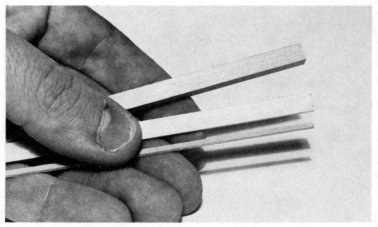

Fig. 3-5. Scale lumber comes in long sizes. From top to bottom are a scale 6x12, 2x12 and 2x4.

Table 3-1. O, HO Scale and Fractional Lumber Sizes.

ACTUAL SIZE	COMPARISON SIZE	O	S	OO	HO	TT	N	Z
0.0115	1″ (HO)	½	¾	⅞	1	1⅜	1⅞	2½
0.0208	1″ (O)	1	1⅜	1⅝	1¾	2½	3⅜	4⅝
0.0230	2″ (HO)	1⅛	1½	1¾	2	2¾	3⅝	5
0.0312	1/32″	1½	2	2⅜	2¾	3¾	5	6⅞
0.0344	3″ (HO)	1⅝	2¼	2⅝	3	4⅛	5½	7½
0.0394	1mm	1⅞	2½	3	3⅜	4¾	6¼	8⅝
0.0417	2″ (HO)	2	2⅝	3⅛	3⅝	5	6⅝	9⅛
0.0459	4″ (HO)	2¼	3	3½	4	5½	7⅜	10⅛
0.0469	¾	2¼	3	3½	4	5⅝	7½	10¼
0.0625	1/16″ & 3″ (O)	3	4	4¾	5½	7½	10	13¾
0.0689	6″ (HO)	3¼	4⅜	5¼	6	8¼	11	15⅛
0.0781	5/64	3¾	5	6	6¾	9⅜	12½	17¼
0.0833	4″ (O)	4	5⅜	6⅜	7¼	10	13⅜	18⅜
0.0916	8″ (HO)	4⅜	5⅞	7	8	11	14¾	20¼
0.0938	3/32	4½	6	7⅛	8⅛	11¼	15	20⅝
0.1148	10″ (HO)	5½	7⅜	8¾	10	13¾	18⅜	25¼
0.1250	⅛ & 6″ (O)	6	8	9½	10⅞	15	20	27½
0.1378	12″ (HO)	6⅝	8⅞	10½	12	16½	22	30¼
0.1560	5/32	7½	10	11⅞	13⅝	18¾	25	34⅜
0.1608	14″ (HO)	7¾	10¼	12¼	14	19¼	25¾	35⅜
0.1667	8″ (O)	8	10⅝	12¾	14½	20	26⅝	36⅝
0.1837	16″ (HO)	8⅞	11¾	14	16	22	29⅜	40⅜
0.1880	3/16	9	12	14½	16⅜	22½	30	41¼
0.1970	5mm	9½	12⅝	15	17⅛	23⅝	31½	43¼
0.2067	18″ (HO)	9⅞	13¼	15¾	18	24¾	33	45½
0.2083	10″ (O)	10	13⅜	15⅞	18⅛	25	33⅜	45⅞
0.2296	20″ (HO)	11	14¾	17½	20	27½	36¾	50½
0.2500	¼ & 12″ (O)	12	16	19	21¾	30	40	55
0.2526	22″ (HO)	12⅛	16⅛	19¼	22	30¼	40⅜	55½
0.2756	24″ (O)	13¼	17⅛	21	24	33	44	60⅝
0.2917	14″ (O)	14	18⅝	22¼	25⅜	35	46⅝	64⅛
0.3120	5/16	15	20	23¾	27¼	37½	50	68¾
0.3333	16″ (O)	16	21⅜	25⅜	29	40	53⅜	73⅜
0.3750	⅜ & 18″ (O)	18	24	28⅝	32⅝	45	60	82½
0.3940	10mm	18⅞	25¼	30	34¼	47¼	63	86⅝
0.4167	20″ (O)	20	26⅝	31¾	36¼	50	66⅝	91⅝
0.4380	7/16	21	28	33⅜	38	52½	70	96¼
0.4583	22″ (O)	22	29⅜	34⅞	39⅞	55	73⅜	100⅞
0.5000	½ & 24″ (O)	24	32	38⅛	43½	60	80	110
0.7500	¾	36	48	57⅛	65¼	90	120	165
1.0000	1	48	64	76¼	87⅛	120	160	220

All dimensions given in scale inches to nearest ⅛ of a scale inch.

These handy tables offer a quick means to convert strip-wood sizes to scale lumber dimensions, or convert scale lumber sizes from one scale to another

don't like to work with a soldering gun. Be careful cutting and working with these very fragile materials.

Sheet Stock

The thought of individually gluing on every board in a huge house may just be too much for many of us. The manufacturers have come to our aid with large sheets of premilled siding in a variety of styles. Thin sheets usually 1/32″ or 1/16″ thick, 2-4″ wide, and

Table 3-2. O Scale Lumber.

O	S		OO		HO		TT		N		Z	
1	1.33	1⅜	1.59	¾	1.81	1¾	2.50	2½	3.33	3⅜	4.58	4⅝
2	2.67	2⅝	3.18	3⅛	3.63	3⅝	5.00	5	6.67	6⅝	9.17	9⅛
3	4.00	4	4.76	4¾	5.44	5½	7.50	7½	10.00	10	13.75	13¾
4	5.33	5⅜	6.35	6⅜	7.26	7¼	10.00	10	13.33	13⅜	18.33	18⅜
6	8.00	8	9.52	9½	10.88	10⅞	15.00	15	20.00	20	27.50	27½
8	10.67	10⅝	12.70	12¾	14.51	14½	20.00	20	26.67	26⅝	36.67	36⅝
10	13.33	13⅜	15.88	15⅞	18.14	18⅛	25.00	25	33.33	33⅜	45.83	45⅞
12	16.00	16	19.05	19	21.77	21¾	30.00	30	40.00	40	55.00	55
14	18.67	18⅝	22.22	22¼	25.40	25⅜	35.00	35	46.67	46⅝	64.17	64⅛
16	21.33	21⅜	25.40	25⅜	29.03	29	40.00	40	53.33	53⅜	73.33	73⅜
18	24.00	24	28.58	28⅝	32.66	32⅝	45.00	45	60.00	60	82.50	82½
20	26.67	26⅝	31.75	31¾	36.28	36¼	50.00	50	66.67	66⅝	91.67	91⅝
22	29.33	29⅜	34.92	34⅞	39.91	39⅞	55.00	55	73.33	73⅜	100.83	100⅞
24	32.00	32	38.10	38⅛	43.54	43½	60.00	60	80.00	80	110	110

Read the O scale lumber size in the first column (available in hobby shops), then move to the columns for your scale: The first gives the scale equivalence in a decimal form, the second in a fractional form to the nearest ⅛ of a scale inch.

have a typical structural surface milled into them. Various styles include clapboard, planking, random planking, board, and batten, among others. These are most useful for structures with large surface areas (Fig. 3-6).

SELECTING AND STORING WOOD

If you are at all serious about scratchbuilding structures, begin *now* to build up a virtual lumber yard of wood. I generally buy about three times the lumber I need for a model to keep the wood pile filled for those little projects that are fun but don't merit a trip to the hobby shop. At times the lumber supply has been sporadic and having your own stockpile will prevent any disappointments.

To store my lumber I've built a little rack made from an old paneling display stand to hold the various sizes of lumber (Fig. 3-7). The upright open design allows me to keep a close watch on the supply, use even short scrap pieces, and re-order when the supply gets low (Fig. 3-8).

I prefer to select my wood in person if at all possible. Check a few randomly selected pieces at both ends and in the middle with a small ruler or, better yet, a caliper to see that the cross section is uniform. Beware of wood with very heavy fuzz or saw swirls. These may look innocent but will cause you hours of sanding to

Table 3-3. HO Scale Lumber.

HO	O		S		OO		TT		N		Z	
1	0.55	½	0.73	¾	0.87	⅞	1.34	1⅜	1.84	1⅞	2.53	2½
2	1.10	1⅛	1.47	1½	1.75	1¾	2.76	2¾	3.67	3⅝	5.05	5
3	1.65	1⅝	2.20	2¼	2.62	2⅝	4.13	4⅛	5.51	5½	7.58	7½
4	2.20	2¼	2.94	3	3.50	3½	5.51	5½	7.35	7⅜	10.10	10⅛
6	3.31	3¼	4.40	4⅜	5.24	5¼	8.27	8¼	11.02	11	15.15	15⅛
8	4.41	4⅜	5.87	5⅞	7.00	7	11.02	11	14.70	14¾	20.20	20¼
10	5.51	5½	7.34	7⅜	8.74	8¾	13.78	13¾	18.37	18⅜	25.25	25¼
12	6.61	6⅝	8.81	8⅞	10.49	10½	16.54	16½	22.04	22	30.30	30¼
14	7.71	7¾	10.28	10¼	12.25	12¼	10.29	19¼	25.72	25¾	35.35	35⅜
16	8.82	8⅞	11.74	11¾	13.98	14	22.05	22	29.39	29⅜	40.40	40⅜
18	9.92	9⅞	13.21	13¼	15.73	15¾	24.80	24¾	33.07	33	45.45	45½
20	11.02	11	14.68	14¾	17.48	17½	27.56	27½	36.74	36¾	50.50	50½
22	12.12	12⅛	16.15	16⅛	19.23	19¼	30.32	30¼	40.41	40⅜	55.55	55½
24	13.22	13¼	17.62	17⅛	20.98	21	33.07	33	44.09	44	60.60	60⅝

Read the HO scale lumber size in the first column (available in hobby shopes), then move to the columns for your scale: The first gives the scale equivalence in a decimal form, the second in fractional form to the nearest ⅛ of a scale inch.

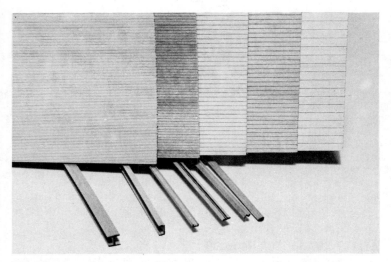

Fig. 3-6. At the bottom are special wooden shapes available from most large hobby shops. From left to right are an "H" column, large and small channels, doortrack, Z-bracing and quarter round stock. The sheet stock above is a milled surface in a thin piece of wood. Included are two sizes of scribed sheeting, clapboard, plus board and batten stock.

remove them from the finished product. In selecting sheet wood be cautious of large dark areas or course grains that run across the wood. The sheet is actually supposed to represent many individual boards ganged together so a continuous course grain that runs directly across the piece destroys the image of individual boards. Sanding in between the boards is just not the answer. Select the clearest, straightest pieces with the least grain possible.

COLORING WOOD

There are two basic methods for coloring wood: stain and paint. Paint contains a pigment and vehicle that literally covers the wood with a coating of color. Stains, on the other hand, are colored but not opaque and allow the grain to easily show through.

Many varieties of hobby paints are available; among these, Floquil is ths most common. Most have a solvent base but some such as Floquil's Poly-S are water-based. Model paints have finely ground pigments to prevent hiding details, so it's generally best to use two or three light coats rather than one heavy one. As stated earlier, basswood will raise a stiff grain after the first painting. Fine sandpaper can be used to remove this grain before the second coat and this results in a very smooth finish. For rough wood structures and older buildings, the fuzz can actually enhance the "aging" of the building.

As a general rule, I pre-paint all my wood material *before* cutting and assembly, especially if more than one color is involved. It's almost impossible to paint a piece of model trimwork a contrasting color after the model has been assembled. You don't want every piece to have exactly the same "new" looking color. Many modelers use a pad—wiping method to give different tones and hues. Take a small pad of cloth or toweling and add a large dab of paint. Holding the pad between your thumb and forefinger, draw the piece of stripwood or stock through the pad while varying the pressure just a bit. As the paint is consumed, the darkness and character of the coloring will change. Try to produce a stock that is similar in color but subtly different. On larger sheets, the pad may be used to wipe across the wood but always follow the grain rather than cross it.

Fig. 3-7. This simple wood rack acts as my "lumberyard." Each size of wood has its own place. The crosspieces or "keepers" are spaced to allow access to both short and long pieces, thus minimizing waste.

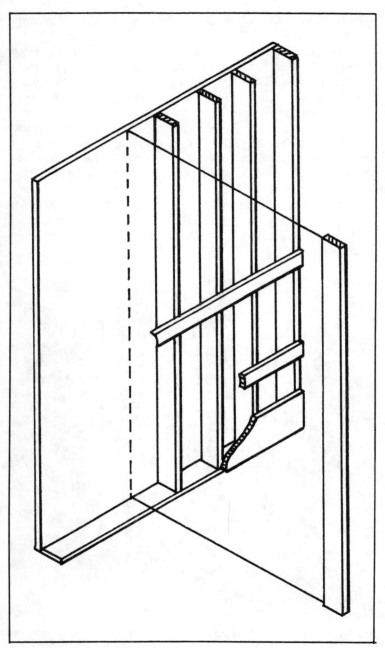

Fig. 3-8. Strip wood rack (not to scale).

A second method for weathering wood is called "dry brushing". As wood ages, paint will flake and fall away in large chunks. Although there are other advanced techniques, the easiest is to dip a brush in the chosen color, then wipe off much of the paint until the bristles are nearly dry. With sort of a scrubbing action, brush the surface, trying not to completely cover with the chosen color. The effect should be one of a blotched, peeled surface. The method works best with wood that has already been stained a light gray, then dry brushed, and finally dulled with a second wash of stain. As with most weathering, too little is better than too much.

Stains are more subtle and are used for weathering or aging models. Many different colors are available from Floquil. The most common stain that I use is either a light or dark flat black. Aging tends to dull all paints and give unpainted wood a sort of silver gray tone. I therefore liberally wash all my models with at least a dulling coat of gray stain to kill the new look of fresh paint. An inexpensive stain can be made by adding a few drops of black shoe dye (*not* shoe polish) to ordinary rubbing alcohol. The amount is a matter of personal preference, but too little is better than too much since you can always add more dye. I usually make up a pint or so which will last for several years. After a while, some of the solids will settle to the bottom so you actually will have a choice of stains from the same bottle—take from the bottom for a dark stain, from the top for a light one. Be careful of shoe dyes. Some are actually very dark blue rather than true black. On your shoes it makes no difference, but diluted on the model . . . well, a light blue bridge is not very realistic.

The same approach should be used in staining as in painting. Prestain each piece a slightly different color before cutting. By flowing on the stain and blowing just a bit, the solvent will quickly evaporate and leave a layer of dark specks that nicely simulates dust and dirt. This technique can be used at the base of buildings, or in doorways and other areas where dirt is likely to collect.

As with all solvent-based materials, be sure to use paints and stains in a well-ventilated area. Your health should be a first priority.

Another caution—since stains are largely solvent, they will be quickly absorbed into the wood itself. For stripwood this is no problem, but if you are weathering or aging an entire wall, the chances for warping and buckling are very real. The structure must have sufficient bracing to prevent the warpage (Fig. 3-9).

To prevent paints from drying out, seal the caps tightly and store them upside down. With solids at the cap, no air can enter and

Fig. 3-9. A top view of this building reveals the heavy bracing inside the sheetwood walls to provide strength and prevent warping from stain solvents.

paints last much longer. Stored in *any* position the pigment will settle. To aid in mixing I add ten pieces of medium size lead shot pellets or BB's. When the bottle is shaken, the shot helps to mix the pigment.

GLUES, ADHESIVES AND JOINTS

When dealing with wood there is generally only one type of glue used—white glue. Available from many manufacturers under the name Elmer's, Ambroid, or School Glue, just to name a few, it is an organic material in a water base that forms a polymer when dry and makes a waterproof bond. There are several variations on the basic theme, with Carpenter's glue having a little more tack or initial holding power and the ability to be sanded when dry. The less expensive glues tend to curl, tear or crack when sanded.

As with any adhesive, the strength is in a thin film of contact rather than the glue itself. Use a *thin* coating rather than a large amount, and press the pieces *tightly* together. This technique will minimize glue oozing out of the joint and make a tight joint without gaps. Clamp, press with weights, or just hold until the glue has fully set—usually a minimum of 20 minutes. It is not however necessary to delay your project while the glue dries. Get in the habit of doing several sub-assemblies or different aspects of the project at the same time. While the glue on one joint is drying, be setting up another, staining more wood, or sanding previously set joints. In modeling we do cheat at times and do not follow the exact prototype practice. For example, you will seldom find a real butt joint—the end of one board attached directly to another (Fig. 3-10). Structurally this is very weak. The prototype would use a lap joint or a mortise and tenon—a sort of hole and tooth joint. In modeling, we don't need the strength, so butt joints are common. The problem is that the end of the board exposes the open grain of the wood to the cement. Being water-based, white glue is quickly drawn into the wood and away from the joint. Many modelers just increase the amount of glue. This *can* be successful, but usually results in a glue—smeared joint. I use a two-step approach to avoid the problem. After cutting the wood to size and checking to see that it properly fits, I apply a liberal coating of glue to the end of the board and allow it to be drawn into the grain and dry, actually sealing the end. Then a second light coating is applied, and the two pieces of wood joined and clamped until dry. The result is a strong,

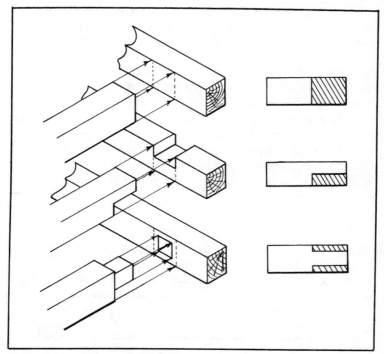

Fig. 3-10. Joint styles (not to scale).

Table 3-4. Suggested Glue Usage.

	Wood	Paper	Plastic	Glass	Metal	Plaster
White Glue	E	G	P	P	P	E
Epoxy	G	G	G	E	E	G
ACC*	P	P	E	E	E	P
Contact Cement	E	E	G	E	E	P
Plastic Cement (Thick)	P	E	E	P	P	G
Plastic Liquid Glues (Thin)	P	P	E	P	P	P

E = Excellent
G = Good
P = Poor
* Alpha Cyanoacrylates or "Super Glues" Some newer formulations may be usable with wood.

clean joint. Remember that this double gluing method is *only* necessary for butt joints.

Although the butt joint is frequently used in model construction, in some cases a slight modification will provide for a better joint. It may be difficult to cut the trim piece to an exact dimension and perfectly square at the same time. Many times it winds up a little too long or just a shade too short, leaving an obvious gap. In those cases where strength is not important, such as a laminated piece of trim over a scribed sheetwood base, the wood may be cut at a slight angle away from the joint (Fig. 3-11). This is a much more forgiving joint without actually making that "perfect cut."

Glues and adhesives come in many different forms and compositions, but the general rule is that the best joints are those with a large contact area, high pressure while setting, and a

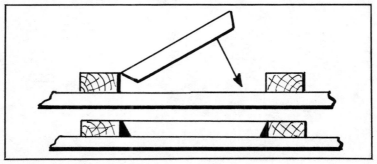

Fig. 3-11. Press fit joint.

minimum of glue. It's not the glue that makes the joint, but the union of each side of the joint by a film of adhesive. For model work, most glue applicators are crude and oversized. Even when only a small hole is made in the top of a glue bottle, it tends to dry and clog and there will be times when a good dab of glue will be necessary. I've completely given up on special glue guns that clog and pins in the tips of glue tubes. Instead, the easiest, though slightly wasteful, solution is to commandeer a discarded flexible top from a plastic margarine tub. Most glues (including some epoxies) will not adhere to the plastic surface. It's an easy task to squeeze out a dollop of glue into the plastic top; then use a pin, small nail, or a scrap piece of wood to apply the glue. The more adhesive needed, the larger the applicator. I like to run a bead of glue down the edge of the piece to be attached, then spread it into a thin film with my finger. There should be enough glue to just spread and make contact but *not* ooze from the joint. Be careful with the fast-acting "super glues" and cyanoacrylates, since they will almost instantly glue your finger to the work piece as well. Once the unused glue has dried, the solid mass can easily be removed from the plastic top by flexing.

Table 3-2 gives a general idea of what types of adhesives to use with different materials.

CUTTING TECHNIQUES

A knife itself may be used to mark the wood for the cut. The cutting action should be with a downward slice rather than a straight push. When cutting a large piece of sheetwood, the cut should be made with several repetitive cuts. Go over and over the same line. Cutting a 1/16″ thick piece of sheetwood will take 8-12 strokes. Always use a metal straightedge when cutting a modeling material. Your hand is simply not steady enough to make a realistically straight line of any length. If at all possible, position the ruler to cover the piece of material you want to save. In this fashion, if the knife slips or wanders it will cut into the scrap, *not* your good piece. The special shapes such as I-beams will split if any cutting pressure is applied. These should be filled with scrap wood as supports and the entire "sandwich" cut through. (Fig. 3-12). Frequently replace blades to always keep a sharp cutting edge.

LAYOUT AND CONSTRUCTION TECHNIQUES

To help eliminate cutting frustration, use a wall or object already cut out as the pattern for another part of the model. For

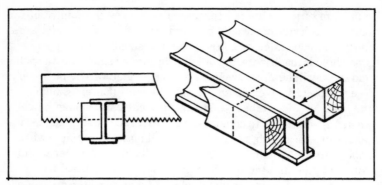

Fig. 3-12. Cutting structural shapes.

example, if you are making a small house with the usual peaked gable, lay out one wall on your stock and cut it out. Rather than measure and lay out the facing wall, use the *first* wall piece as a pattern for the other wall. Be sure to turn it over, though, as the wood pattern must be on the outside. Copying one wall from the other will insure that they are identical . . . maybe not a perfect copy of the plans, but identical nevertheless. Our goal should be for a model that looks perfect if it cannot actually be perfect.

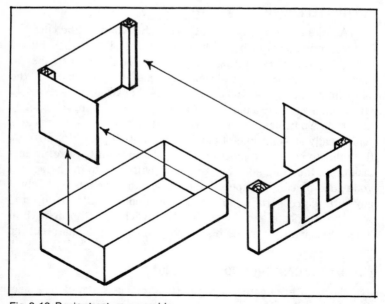

Fig. 3-13. Basic structure assembly.

Most wooden structures are made from a box-like shell with sheetwood walls and solid pieces of wood for corner support. Many modelers build up the walls to near completion before assembling into the box, since it's easier to work with a flat wall on the workbench until completely finished. The final assembly *must* be square and perpendicular to the base. If you assemble the walls sequentially in kind of a circle, it's quite possible small errors in alignment will keep adding together so your last joint will be grossly out of line.

It's better to assemble the walls in sets of two, each forming a sort of L-shaped section. Carefully glue a large piece of corner bracing to one end of each wall. Check the ends so none will overlap when the full structure is made. Hold the wall upright or against a

Fig. 3-14. This small shanty has plenty of bracing for support. The walls are made by laminating or layering the wood parts over a base of thin plastic.

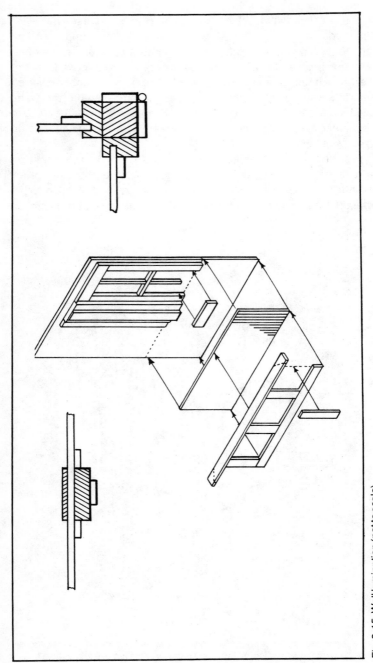

Fig. 3-15. Wall lamination (not to scale).

large flat object so the brace will be exactly flush with your wall—not extending over, not short. Clamp and allow to thoroughly dry. Take two of the wall sections and glue together in an old cigar box or similar strong box and use one of the corners as a fixture or guide to assure that the corners are square and upright. Hold in place with weights and clamps until dry. Finally assemble the two L-sections into the completed box. Again clamp and check and recheck for square. Once the glue has set it's too late to correct errors (Fig. 3-13). Prototype construction usually employs a stud wall—2x4's and other wood pieces to which sheathing or siding is attached. Except in the rarest cases this is seldom used in modeling. For contest modeling it might be possible but in most circumstances, the wall interiors are never seen and a much simplified approach is taken. The primary method is one of *lamination*. A base material, usually scribed sheetwood (although clear plastic may be a good alternative), is laminated with a series

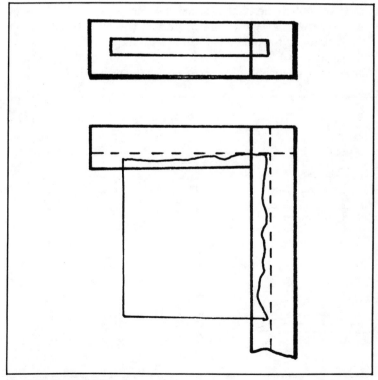

Fig. 3-16. Door track framing.

of layers of stripwood to form the final wall surface. If a large number of windows is present, a thin but strong sheet of clear plastic may be used as the base for the entire side; the wall, windows and framing are built up right on top of it. A good example is the shanty in Fig. 3-14. With the plastic base, all the windows are exactly straight and parallel. Placing tiny windows into the structure would be almost impossible. Lamination will take a bit of thinking on your part, since it completely deviates from the normal construction techniques, but the results are well worth the effort (Fig. 3-15).

Door track or channel is a very convenient piece of commercially available stock to use in window and door construction. Basically a piece of stripwood with a narrow slot cut along one side, it can be used to hold window glass. By tucking the edge into the channel a perfect cut along the glass need not be made (Fig. 3-16).

No one is perfect. No matter how hard you may try, it is seldom that you'll cut a piece of wood exactly straight or that a corner or joint is perfectly square. I can say this from years of experience with very few, if any, perfect corners. The judicious use of trim can completely eliminate the error. Timing is important, however. Corner trim may be simulated by using a square piece of stripwood and butt joining the wall to it (Fig. 3-17).

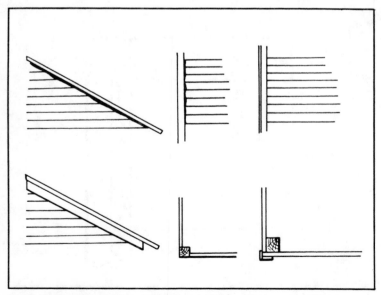

Fig. 3-17. Using trim to hide rough edges (not to scale).

Fig. 3-18. The trim pieces on the walls of the shanty were deliberately left long, then cut back to the exact size of the model, rather than cut from a plan.

This requires a perfectly straight cut on the wall. By gluing the wall together first, then placing the trim *over* the joint, a ragged joint may be completely hidden. The same is true for trim along the roof line. Glue the roof on first, then slide the trim up next to it and as tight as possible under the eave. The trim will hide any flaws in the roof line. Gluing the trim on first will require a perfect roof line, which is unlikely. The same approach may be used at windows and doors. In some models, I've added extra trim just to hide my mistakes.

Another aspect of construction that may be helpful is to try and cut your pieces *directly* to fit your model as often as possible, rather than *indirectly* from the plans. For example, the window sills in the shanty model were deliberately left a little longer than needed (Fig. 3-18). Later they were trimmed back when the building was assembled to a near perfect fit. It's unlikely this good a fit could be made by cutting the sills to size directly from the plans. Also, when trimming your oversized pieces be certain you have a scrap chunk of wood or some form of support behind the trimmed piece. It does take some pressure, and a snapped off detail can be very disappointing.

That about concludes our discussion. Let's now go on to some actual construction projects in wood.

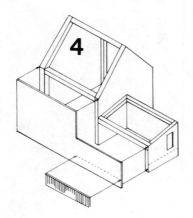

Building A Simple
Drainage Bridge

The railroads cut their way across the prairies and mountains to unite the nation in the 1860's. Surveyors laid out the most direct paths through the flatlands and most advantageous routes in the tortuous elevations. But even on level terrain, one constant enemy is water. It can soften and shift roadbeds, damage rails, upset electrical connections, and just be a general nuisance. To avoid the water problem, roadbeds are contoured, ditched, ballasted, tiled, and drained to funnel the offending moisture away. The problem is universal. I remember driving along the flat prairies of Illinois once and counting over forty bridges, culverts, tiles, and channels in a thirty mile segment of the Illionis Central Railroad. Bridges are, of course, a real blessing for the modeler since there is nothing more boring than miles (well, maybe feet) of flat track between towns or industries. Bridges and culverts can break up the spacing, increase the illusion of distance, and offer a chance to construct some dandy items that are especially designed for your layout (Figs. 4-1 through 4-3).

This may be the first scratchbuilding project for some of you, so I've detailed the construction with kit-like instructions. You supply the material, tools and enthusiasm. Let's begin.

The prototype for this model is on the Chicago and Northwestern RR in Union, Illinois about 60 miles northwest of Chicago (Figs. 4-4 through 4-7). It's just a few yards from the western terminal of the Illinois Railway Museum right-of-way over a little stream. Because of its small size and relative simplicity, I believe

Fig. 4-1. A simple drainage bridge that you can build.

this bridge is just the thing for a first-time project. In some places I've supplied alternative construction methods. Remember, the easier route may produce an acceptable model but if you want to improve your skills, try the more detailed way . . . at least once in a while. The project is mostly wood with a steel underframe that is

Fig. 4-2. The model is diminutive, but an interesting detail that can be added to any layout. Added details like the small nut-bolt-washer (NBW) castings and tie plates make the model special.

Fig. 4-3. The model drainage bridge spans a dry gully.

simulated in plastic. If you don't want to try scratchbuilding in plastic, that's fine; just replace the 12 inch steel I-beams with wooden 12 x 6's. I'm sure this just follows an older prototype design.

Begin by purchasing the necessary scale lumber indicated in the bill of materials (Table 4-1). I usually buy two to three times the amounts actually used for a project to build up a supply for future needs. A key point is to prestain each long piece a weathered gray *before* cutting to size. Try to wash each piece with a little more or

Fig. 4-4. Prototype in Union, Illinois on the Chicago and Northwestern R.R. branch.

76

Fig. 4-5. Only about 25 feet long, the model will take only a small space on the layout yet add extra interest.

less stain to produce a variation in the coloring (Fig. 4-8). I use a wash of rubbing alcohol and black shoe dye (not polish) for weathering. The proportion isn't important; just a lot of alcohol to a little dye. Some modelers prefer commercial products such as Weather-it, or the various weathering colors direct from the paint manufacturers. Many just save a bottle of thinner and clean all their brushes in it. The spent thinner makes a great wash.

Fig. 4-6. Notice the many boltheads and the rough texture of the lumber.

Fig. 4-7. The bridge rests on a limestone or sandstone set of piers. On the model, these are simulated with broken pieces of plaster.

Study the drawings (Figs. 4-9 through 4-11) and photographs carefully. Decide for yourself how you would go about beginning construction. Compare that to my suggestions. Maybe your way is better, maybe not. Ask why I chose the sequence of construction. Would things go together in a better or more convenient way? Now you're thinking like a scratchbuilder. Let's get on with some building.

Table 4-1. Bill of Materials.

Chicago and Northwestern R.R. Bridge Union, Illinois			
SCALE LUMBER*		HARDWARE*	
Scale Feet			
200	8"×8"	26 Tie plates	
50	3"×10"	6 Large nut-bolt-washers	
40	6"×8"	50 Small nut-bolt-washers	
40	8"×12"		
120	2"×10"	MISCELLANEOUS	
175	2"×4"		
50	3"×2"	72' 12" I-beam	
50	9"×2"	or	
100	12"×12"	72' 6×12 wood beams	
		5 Square inch 0.015 stryene sheet or scrap wood to shim under beams	

*Many of these materials come in stock sizes or packages. Buy in excess for future projects. Some sizes of lumber are not available in all scales so come as close as reasonable.

78

Use your scale rule to transfer drawing dimensions to your wood. These may differ slightly from the dimensions quoted in text, since there will always be a slight printing error in any published plans (as much as 3-5%) and some reading error on your part. The most easily read plans are those in the largest scales. I generally make my own plans in ⅜ or ½ inch to the foot scales. These are quite large, but offer little problem in reading with a proper scale rule. Plans printed in N or Z scale have line widths that approach scale inches in dimension. Never complain if a magazine or publisher doesn't publish plans in your scale but in the less common but larger scales. He's actually doing you a great favor, since transferring dimensions from an O scale plan to an N scale model will be much more accurate than from an N scale plan to N scale model. If you feel terribly uncomfortable in doing all the ruler

Fig. 4-8. The basic building material is scale lumber cut to length with a razor saw. All pieces are prestained with a very dilute wash of black shoe dye in alcohol. Notice how the different pieces have a slightly different coloration.

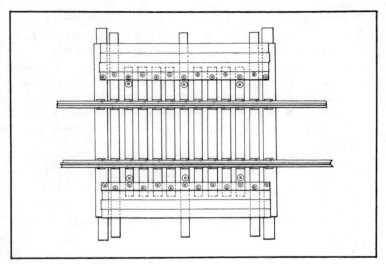

Fig. 4-9. Drainage bridge—top view (HO scale).

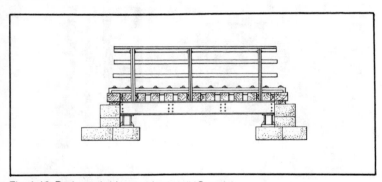

Fig. 4-10. Drainage bridge—side view (HO scale).

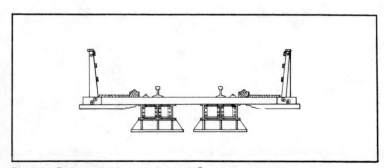

Fig. 4-11. Drainage bridge—end view (HO scale).

gymnastics, then take your plan to a blueprint shop and have them reproduce it in your scale. Make a few Xerox copies to protect the original from cuts and glue blobs and just jump in. A set of twin pointed dividers can be used to transfer each dimension directly—no rulers, no reading.

UNION BRIDGE-CONSTRUCTION

1. Prestain all wooden parts a weathered gray. Try *not* to make pieces look similar.

2. From 8 x 8 stock cut 8 pieces 10' 2" long and 3 pieces 16' 2" long. Sand and stain the ends. These are the bridge ties or *deck*. Bundle with rubber band and mark size.

3. Cut 2 pieces 6" x 8" x 20' and 6 pieces 2" x 10" x 12' 10". Sand and stain the ends. Bundle and mark. These are guard timbers and walkway planks.

4. Cut 2 pieces of 8" x 12" x 13' 8" and 2 pieces 3" x 10" x 12' 7". Sand, stain and bundle.

5. Two 6 x 8 beams act as guard rails along the track and over the top of all the bridge ties. Each is notched in about 2 inches for all the ties. The easy way is not to notch the beams at all; use a 4 x 8

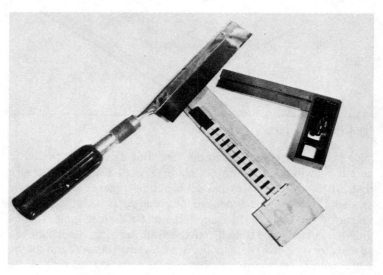

Fig. 4-12. A small fixture or guide was constructed to hold the guard timbers in place while cutting notches for the ties. A small square is used to assure proper location. With the razor saw, two lines are cut at either side of the notch. A very sharp knife cuts out the bulk of the material with a small square file used to finish each hole.

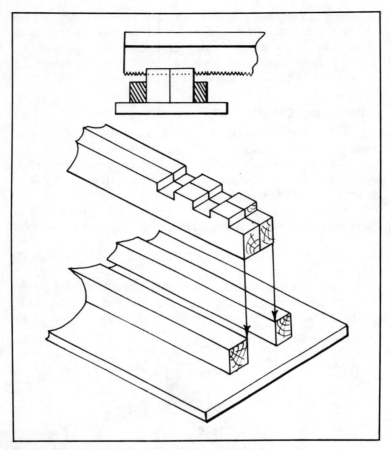

Fig. 4-13. Notching fixture (not to scale).

instead and just glue them to the ties. But if you want the extra detail, we will need a fixture or guide (Figs. 4-12, 4-13) to assure that all the notches are the same depth, square, and properly spaced. It would be best to make the guide out of metal so as not to be cut by the tools, but I made mine of 4 x 4 scale lumber stock glued to a sheetwood base. From the scale drawing, determine the spacing for the notches, mark these with a small square, and cut the edges with a very sharp saw. Remove the excess wood with a knife and finish with a small square file. Each cut and the filing process should not extend below the wood guide. Use a scrap piece of 8 x 8 tie stock to check that the ties will fit snugly in the notches. Start at one end and work across, cutting both timbers at the same time.

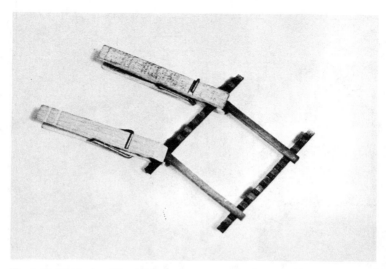

Fig. 4-14. The first and last short ties are attached first. Carefully note that these are *not* in the first and last notches, which are to be used for other timbers.

The 6 x 8 timbers are deliberately extra long so the excess may be trimmed off to 13′ 0″. Had the guard beams been cut to the exact length first, your notch spacing would have to have been perfect—an unlikely occurance even for experts. In this way your spacing

Fig. 4-15. Placing the subassembly against a block of wood allows all the other ties to be aligned without problem. Be sure to clamp and allow to dry completely.

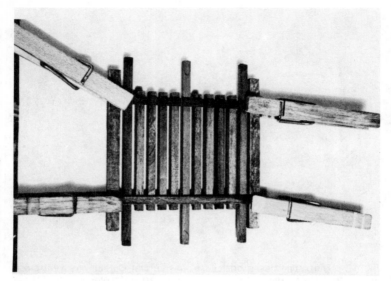

Fig. 4-16. The end timbers are clamped in place. Note how well the ties are aligned.

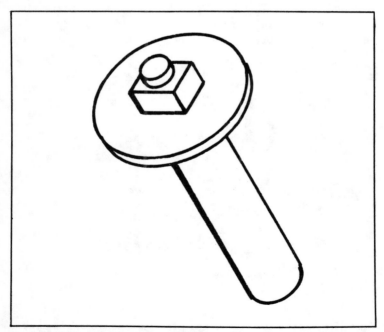

Fig. 4-17. Nut-bolt-washer casting (NBW).

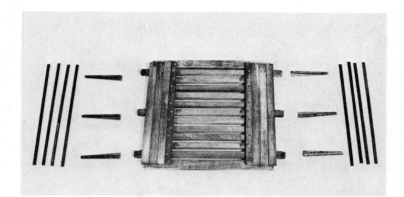

Fig. 4-18. Pieces to make the railings are in place. It would be very difficult to build the railings separately and then attach because the tie spacings are not necessarily perfect. It's therefore a better approach to build the railings right in place.

may vary just a little but the timbers will still line up perfectly. Stain the raw wood.

6. There are 8 short and 3 long 8 x 8 ties. Glue on the first and last short ties to the notched guard timbers (Fig. 4-14), check for square, clamp, and let dry. Using a block of wood or metal bar as a

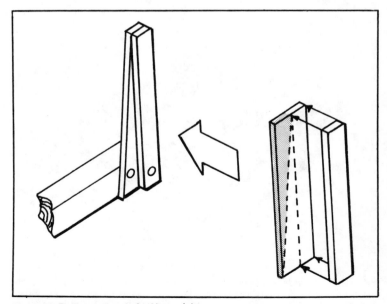

Fig. 4-19. Railing supports (not to scale).

Fig. 4-20. The square again assures good alignment while the clothes pin will hold the upright in place while drying.

stop, attach the other short timbers (Fig. 4-15). The wood block assures that all the ties are even.

7. Repeat Step 6 with the longer 8 x 8 ties. Had these long ties been attached first, the smaller ties could not have been aligned with a block.

Fig. 4-21. The bridge rests on two sets of 12″ I-beams, which in this case are plastic material. Ordinary wood 6″x12″ beams could be substituted. Small spacers were used to keep the separation constant.

8. Glue on the 8 x 12 end timbers. Clamp until dry (Fig. 4-16).

9. Glue and clamp the 2 x 10 walk planking. Vary the position and spacing just slightly to emphasize the individual pieces.

10. Prepaint the nut-bolt and washer (NBW) castings (Fig. 4-17) a rusty brown. (Mix a little "boxcar red" in with a stock "rust" colored paint.) Pre-drill holes for the castings in the ties and guard timbers. Attach each with a small amount of glue.

11. The rails are regular stock, except I used Grandt Line plastic tie plates with four spikes per tie. Driving spikes can be tricky business and one slip would ruin your bridge, so I pre-drilled a pilot hole for each spike on the bridge. As an alternative, the rails may be glued in place with epoxy cement.

12. It would be nearly impossible to assemble the railings separately and then attach them to the exact spacing of the long timbers, so these will be built in place (Fig. 4-18). To form the railings, cut 6 pieces of 2 x 9 and 6 of 2 x 3, all 4' 2" long. Glue these together and trim at an angle (Fig. 4-19). Remember, on each side you will need one brace that is cut left to right and two cut right to left. This is so the larger board will always be adjacent to the long support beams. Pre-drill two holes at the base of each support for a small NBW but *do not* put them in place. The irregular shape of the casting will make it impossible to squarely clamp the parts together.

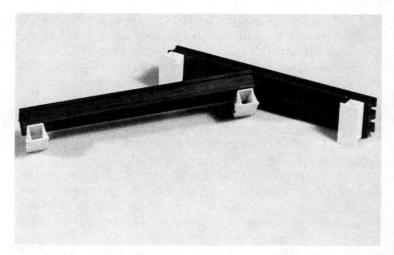

Fig. 4-22. Special plastic pads were made for this bridge following the plans, but wood shims could be easily substituted.

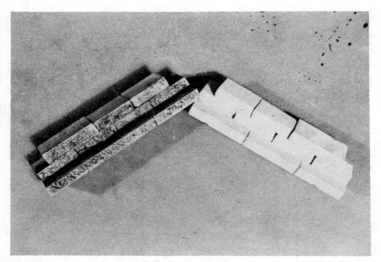

Fig. 4-23. The foundations or piers are broken pieces of plaster. The unfinished plaster is shown at the right, while a finished pier is on the left. Black chalk dust was brushed on the painted pier to highlight the rough texture.

Dab each support with a little glue and using a small square for alignment, attach each to the long ties inside of the long ties on the bridge. After the glue has set slightly, use a clamp or clothespin to firmly hold the parts together while drying. Repeat the process for each brace (Fig. 4-20). When the pieces are dry, attach the 8 pieces of 2 x 4 railing, attempting to be close in alignment but not necessarily perfect. A little variation is found on most prototypes. Allow the railings to thoroughly dry, then add the NBW's at the base on one or both sides of each long tie. Set the finished wooden portion aside and let's continue work on the foundation and underframing.

13. The scale drawings show the underbody detail of the bridge including iron work. I suggest your purchase either plastic or wood 12″ I-beams for the braces and use wooden blocks for the pads rather than the elaborate metal ones shown. I did build up those pads from small pieces of plastic, but for a first-time project they are a bit too complicated (Figs. 4-21, 4-22). As can be seen from the finished model photos, the underside is barely visible so the compromise is minimal. The six main beams may be glued directly to the bridge. See plan for spacing.

14. The bridge rests on large piers made from rough stone which I simulated from sections of ordinary patching plaster. In an

old cookie sheet or similar flat container, pour a layer of plaster about one scale foot deep and allow to thoroughly dry. Spray the sheet first with a little PAM vegetable oil spray (non-stick cooking spray), a silicone material like a drawer lubricant, or Scotchgard water repellent. The coating will allow the plaster to be removed more easily. Scribe the plaster sheet with a knife into strips about three scale feet wide and snap off several pieces. The edges of these broken pieces have a coarse, rough hewn texture. Stack several of the broken sheets together to make the piers. Vertical lines may be cut into the edges of the sheets to simulate individual blocks. Paint the piers a light beige (Floquil "mud") to simulate sandstone. Finally, dust the faces with a ground black chalk or charcoal to accent the rough surface (Fig. 4-23).

15. Add your new bridge to your layout, shimming with the remaining wood. Put it up front where visitors will ask where you got it!

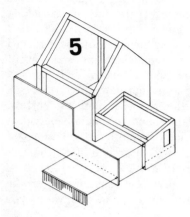

Building The Schulz Brothers' Icehouse

5

It's the summer of 1906 in Springhill, Michigan; the mercury's pushing 95 and only a lazy dog wanders across the dusty streets looking for a cooler place to sleep. Times are quieter and more serene without the commuter rush madness and the mindless drone of air conditioners. Oldtimers rock slowly on rear porches arguing about when it was ever hotter, while down at the railyards an 0-6-0 drifts aimlessly toward the riverfront to switch a string of cars. Several boys try to cool in the river's water but even that is not much use. Possibly the most popular place is the Schulz Brothers' Icehouse on River Street. During the deep of winter, men with specially designed tools cut large blocks of ice from the frozen river and lake to be moved to the icehouse for storage. The blocks, now slightly smaller for their wait, are removed from their slumber to cool drinks and refrigerate the food of Springhills' more affluent citizens. Of course the everpresent kids are around, looking for a dropped piece of ice or just a chance to stand near the big door when it slides open with a breathtaking rush of wet, cool air (Figs. 5-1, 5-2).

Most modelers (myself included) are not true students of architectural design, although we can all appreciate the dramatic changes that have occurred in construction since the turn of the century. Perhaps the greatest difference is the demise of the "gingerbread" designs and ornate buildings of the early 1900's. Study the older buildings in your town. Note the ornate scrollwork, the fancy castings and endless detail. At first they seem a little gauche but a little research shows they reflect the individualism

Fig. 5-1. The Schulz Brother's Ice House will make an interesting addition to any model railroad layout. Only one out-of-focus picture of the prototype was available so I freelanced or estimated the dimensions and general construction techniques.

Fig. 5-2. Although the building is really very plain, the lettering and cupola vent still make it an interesting model.

and enthusiasm of the times—to say nothing of carpentry skills that border on pure art.

At a recent National Model Railroad Association convention I had the opportunity to meet Irv Schulz, who is one of the strongest proponents of "period" or turn of the century modeling. He was kind enough to loan me a part of his old-time Michigan railroad photo collection. A picture of an old ice house in Marquette was especially interesting to me. Because only one rather out of focus photo was available, I freelanced or just estimated the rest of the design and called it—what else—the Schulz Brothers' Ice Company.

Before modern refrigeration, larger blocks of ice were cut from local lakes and rivers and stored in box-like icehouses for summer distribution to individual customers. Generally, the design is simple with no windows, few doors, and a small but ornate roof vent. Although this is far from the filigreed buildings we spoke of before, the commercial advertising posters make the difference. In all humility, The Variety Store boasts "Our prices are the lowest, our assortment the largest." For modelers in HO scale a full set of dry transfers or rub-on lettering is available from Period Graphics, listed as their "barn lettering" set.

Begin construction by laying out the walls of the building on the reverse or back side of scribed sheetwood. Use a sharp, hard pencil and a square to assure a neat final form. Take dimensions from Figures 5-3 through 5-6. Several of the large retailers such as Sears and a few specialty tool houses like the Brookstone Company carry small machinist's squares (4 inches or less) which are very useful for working with the modeling dimensions, where a normal 6-inch square might be cumbersome. Using a sharp modeling knife, cut out the basic wall pieces with many light strokes of the knife rather than a few heavy ones. Always use a straight edge, preferably metal, to guide your cutting strokes. Also position the guide so if the knife should slip it will cut into a waste section, not the good piece you are saving. To cut out the window and door openings, first drill a small hole in each corner of the opening with a drill and pin vice, then cut the opening as before. The drilled corners will eliminate overrun with the knife and give a clean, though slightly rounded corner (Fig. 5-7).

Cutting on the back side of the sheetwood eliminates accidental marks and overruns on the finished surface. Cut one of the peaked ends first, then turn it over and use it as a guide for laying out the other peaked wall.

Fig. 5-3. Schulz Brothers Ice House—back view (N scale).

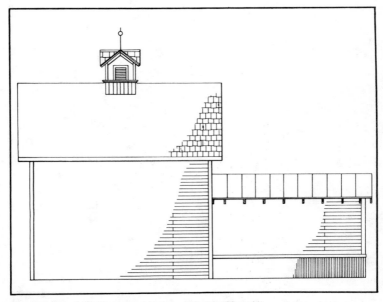

Fig. 5-4. Schulz Brothers Ice House—left side (N scale).

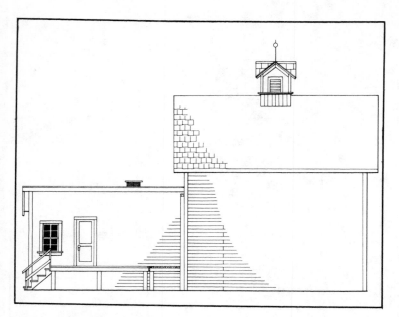

Fig. 5-5. Schulz Brothers Ice House—front view (N scale).

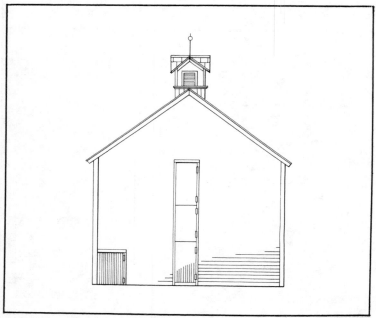

Fig. 5-6. Schulz Brothers Ice House—right side (N scale).

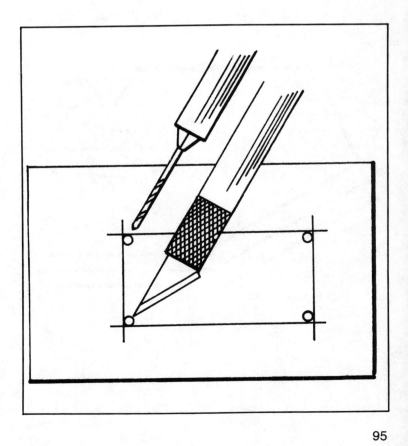

Fig. 5-7. Cutting window openings.

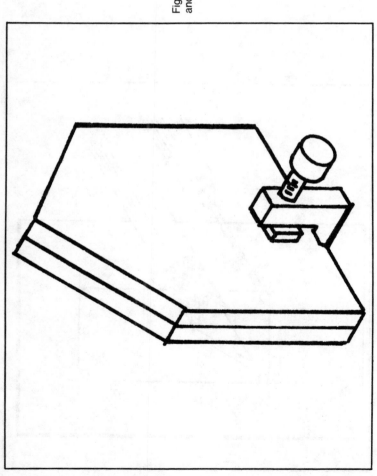

Fig. 5-8. Clamp walls back to back and sand roofline to perfect match.

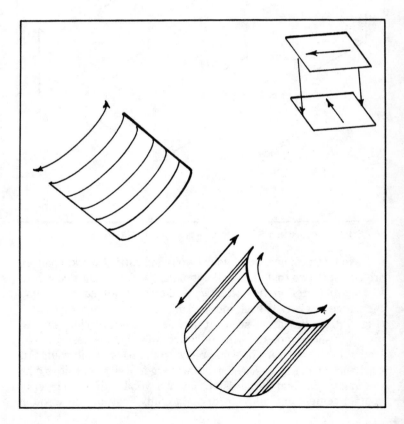

Fig. 5-9. Grain of wood or paper.

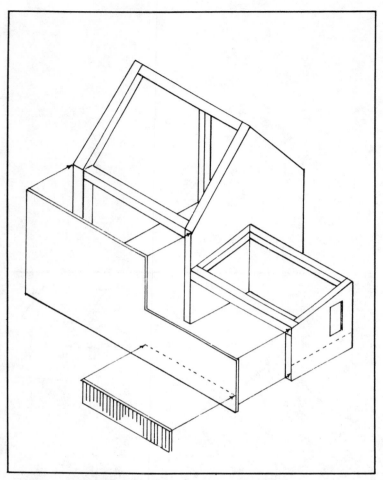

Fig. 5-10. Construction of Schulz Brothers Ice House (not to scale).

No matter how careful your layout and cutting work, chances are good the two roof lines will not match perfectly, thus causing a wobbly roof later on. After the two peaked walls are cut out, clamp them together back to back and sand the roof lines to an exact match (Fig. 5-8). In the larger scales it may be necessary to join several pieces of sheetwood to form the entire wall. This is best done by laminating a cardstock or wood piece to the back of the wall. Cut cardstock pieces at least a quarter inch larger in all dimensions than the wall itself. Coat the cardstock and the wood with a thin layer of contact cement and allow to dry. Carefully position the wood in

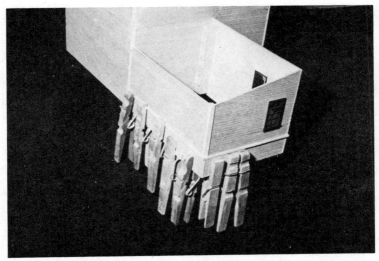

Fig. 5-11. The Wainscot is held in place with a battery of clothes pin clamps until the glue is dry.

place and press to secure. Be careful as the contact cement adheres instantly and there will be little time for adjustment. Be sure the grain of the cardstock or wood backing sheet is perpendicular to the grain of the exterior sheetwood. You can easily find the grain of the

Fig. 5-12. The rear doors are just scribed wood laminated directly over the wall with a frame built around them. Small pieces of wire act as hinges and no effort was made to cut out any openings at all.

Fig. 5-13. Dry transfer lettering available at most art and stationery supply stores was used to do the large lettering. The author's son Tony helps with the project. Do the lettering *before* the walls are assembled into a box.

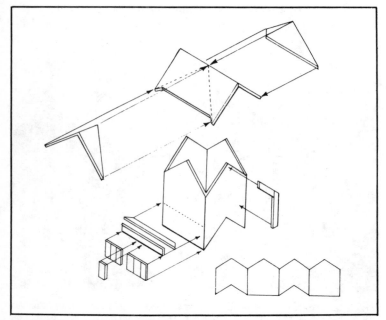

Fig. 5-14. Cupola construction.

Fig. 5-15. The cupola is a special feature of the model and clearly sets it into the circa 1900 period of construction. The ventilator windows were taken directly from a commercial Grandt Line casting. The lightning rod is a pin.

cardstock by flexing a piece in your hand. It will bend more easily in one direction than in the other. The grain runs parallel to the easy flexing direction. Crossing the grains makes for a much more rigid laminate. Be sure to use plenty of heavy weights to hold the

Fig. 5-16. Back view of the completed ice house.

laminates in placed while the glue thoroughly sets. Water-based glues such as Elmer's will cause swelling and warpage and should not generally be used to cement large thin surfaces together (Fig. 5-9). Finally, trim away any excess backing stock.

Many modelers feel it's best to complete as much work as possible on the walls before assembling into the finished form. There are pros and cons to this idea. It does minimize handling, reducing the chance of damage to your fine detail. However, if your walls are not perfectly matched, it may be hard to camouflage the errors when final assembly is complete. Also, weathering with water or solvent based paints cannot be completed since warpage is possible without a good deal of strong bracing.

This model is relatively simple, so I would suggest you assemble the rough walls and detail the box-like base (Fig. 5-10). I use heavy stripwood bracing at the corners, top and bottom of all structures. Strips of ⅛" x ⅛" and ¼" x" are adequate in HO and O scales respectively. Your models hopefully will last for years, and the continuous expanding and contracting through seasonal changes can play havoc with wood models. This will be especially

Fig. 5-17. The finished model could have many additional details, such as ladders to reach the upper doors, some kind of conveyor or lift for moving the ice to the upper lofts, broken boards here and there, more signs and maybe a poster for the circus that's coming to town, some trucks and a rusting old junk car in back . . . the list should only be limited by your imagination.

Fig. 5-18. The completed ice house in its setting on the layout. An attractive and easy-to-make building.

true should you move from a humid climate like Chicago or Houston to an arid one like Arizona or vice versa. Be prepared for some rebuilding and regluing.

The wainscot (vertical base boards) on the office section is a short piece of scribed sheeting glued in place and held with a battery of clothes pins while drying (Fig. 5-11). A piece of 1″ x 3″ trim is added along the top and mitered at the corners. The windows and office door are commercial castings available at most hobby shops. Pick a style that suits your fancy. Add the wall trim, doors, and door trim. With the exception of the office door, all the doors are pieces of scribed sheetwood glued to the wall and then trimmed with scale lumber. The hinges are small bits of wire epoxied in place (Fig. 5-12). Paint the entire structure a light gray such as Floquil's Reefer Gray and weather with a very light grimy black wash or mixture of black shoe dye in alcohol. The company name sign was hand lettered with dry transfer type art lettering (Fig. 5-13). The detailed advertising lettering, which is the heart of this model's appeal, are available in HO scale only from Period Graphics. Send a stamped self-addressed envelope for their latest list of turn of the centry lettering sets (address in Appendix). In other scales a search of old magazines and newspapers might provide adequate sign materials.

The roof is simply a large piece of cardstock slit and folded along the center and glued in place. The roofing material is Campbell glue-backed shingles. A hint here—first glue (using a spray adhesive) a piece of graph paper to your roofing base, then apply the shingles over this. The graph paper will give you a guide to assure that the shingles are straight and don't wander about the roof.

The cupola (Fig. 5-14) offered a special challenge and is a highlight of the model. I laid it out on a single piece of cardstock, scored the corners, and folded it into a box. Check and recheck the roof angles as they may not match the drawings, especially with the shingles in place. Once you are satisfied with the fit, add the trim, ventilators (actually a section cut from Grant Line cast veranda doors), and glue to the roof top. Then add the vertical base boards, one at a time, to fit the roof contour (Fig. 5-15). The roof of the cupola is actually three sections. The first is a small regular roof section going all the way across the top. The second and third are two smaller sections going off to each side. Cut and fit these as before and be prepared to throw away several attempts . . . I did. Once you are finally satisfied, complete the roofing of the cupola with more Campbell shingles. A straight pin is the lightning rod.

Other details include the loading dock made from stripwood and the roof ventilator assembled from several sections of the same Grandt Line cast veranda railing. Study Figs. 5-16 through 5-18 for other detailing ideas.

Many extra details could be added as your time and interest dictates, but this basic ice house model should add an interesting focal point for a hot summer's afternoon on any model scene.

Working with Paper

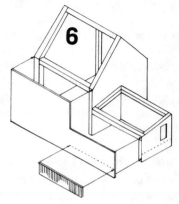

Many modelers have been fortunate to live in an era of fine quality imported brass locomotives, beautiful castings, and an almost unlimited supply of structural shapes, parts, and components. Perhaps we should occasionally remember the "old days" when such a variety of materials was not available. Locomotives were frequently made from light sheet metal stock sometimes salvaged from cans. Cars and structures were often made of cardstock. Not the corrugated box material, but multiple ply laminated sheets.

Paper could be making a comeback in these times of high prices. Cardstock's limited popularity may be from lack of familiarity, rather than a dislike for the material.

Although cardstock has successfully been used to construct all types of models including rolling stock and even interurbans (trolleys), I find it very useful for large area structures. Whether used alone or in combination with other materials, cardstock can be a highly effective modeling medium. My personal choice is a particular brand called Strathmore board, a very high quality paper made in single or multiple plies. Each ply is about .005 inches thick and stocks ranging from one to five plies plus a 1/16" thick illustration board are available. Sheets vary in size up to 30" x 40". When buying stock, be sure to obtain a hard finish surface meant for ink rather than a textured or rough surface used with water colors or pastels. These rough surface boards may have other creative modeling applications—use your imagination. Although more difficult to cut, the thicker stock may be used for structures with minimal interior bracing.

WINDOW AREAS

For models with extensive window and glass areas, a sheet of 1/16" or 1/32" thick plexiglas may be used as the base for the entire wall. Cover the future glass areas with thin masking tape and then proceed to build up the model with layers of cardstock and wood glued directly to the plexiglas. When completely finished (including painting) the tape may be peeled back to reveal the clear window area. This lamination method provides a wall able to support the delicate scale window construction needed in many models where cardstock or wood alone would just not survive even the most careful handling.

SIMULATING WOOD AND METAL

Depending on your final use, cardstock can be finished to simulate wood or metal.

Wood as a porous substance is very similar to cardstock. The yard office in Figs. 6-1 and 6-2 is made almost entirely from scribed cardstock; only the window muntins and porch roof supports are wood. A stain of black shoe dye in rubbing alcohol was used to weather the walls. The proportion is not important; only a little dye to a lot of alcohol. The stock does warp a little as the alcohol is absorbed but this is reversed upon drying. Simulation of only the most coarse wood surfaces will be left unsealed.

To simulate metal or well-painted wood takes a little more work. Since metal is non-porous it is necessary to seal the cardstock, especially the edges. A good automotive body primer or wood sealer/primer can generally be used. This must be sprayed on in three or more very light layers. Brush marks or unsightly runs and sags are just not prototypical. A spray can with an adjustable nozzle is acceptable. Many advanced modelers will eventually purchase an airbrush (Fig. 6-3) which is a mini-paint sprayer with adjustable pattern areas and spray rates. Pressure is supplied by a compressor or tank of compressed gas. Although not a tool for the beginner, an airbrush can eliminate all brush marks and provide very uniform coverage. Paints must be highly thinned for use with an airbrush or problems in flow and surface coverage will develop. If you must use a brush, thin the paint thoroughly and apply several light coats rather than one heavy one. Whatever method you use, it's a good idea to very lightly sand each coat after drying. Use a very fine grit paper—400-600 grit. The sanding will remove any small ridges and extensions of the sealer leaving the

Fig. 6-1. This cardstock model of a yard office is more than 15 years old, yet shows little sign of wear.

valleys to fill. After two or three coats and sandings even a rough surface material will be smooth and sealed like metal.

The oil storage tank in Fig. 6-4 is a wooden block wrapped with a cardstock strip, then sealed, sanded and painted to resemble

Fig. 6-2. Made almost exclusively of cardstock, only the window muntins and porch roof supports are wood. The little awnings over the windows add an extra touch.

Fig. 6-3. An airbrush is nothing more than a mini paint sprayer. Highly diluted paint is held in the bottle and drawn up into the gun by the vacuum action of air rushing through the brush head. Once in the tip, it is broken into tiny droplets and sprayed on the target surface. The painting area and paint flow may be controlled by the operator. Although not a high priority item for beginners, the very smooth surface produced by the airbrush is an asset to any modeler.

metal. Metal construction techniques, especially for older designs, require frequent use of rivets. These may be easily simulated in thin cardstock by pushing in a series of small dimples or raised spots to form the rivet heads. I use a dressmaker's tracing wheel, which is a small disc-type tool with many small points on the edge (Fig. 6-5). Place a soft base like balsa or cardboard under the cardstock, then firmly roll the tracing wheel over the paper. The rivet heads will be uniformly pressed through to the other side. Available at fabric shops, the wheels can be purchased with different spacings and impression sizes. Use a metal ruler to guide the wheel.

Other modelers make rivets individually by drilling a series of holes in a thin brass plate, then pressing the cardstock into the holes with a pencil point. With either method the rivets formed are susceptible to damage. If pressed, they will flatten and partially disappear. When painting, the rivets can be highlighted by rubbing with a light or contrasting paint.

CARDSTOCK CONSTRUCTION TIPS

One ply of strathmore is roughly 0.005 inches. Since an O scale inch is about 0.020 inches and an HO scale is about 0.010 inches, then each ply approximately equals 1/4" O scale and 1/2" HO scale. The scale thickness of any number of plies may be quickly computed.

CUTTING

Cutting cardstock is really quite easy. It is best to *slice*, rather than saw or chop the stock. A very sharp single-edged razor blade is used because it is so thin the blade will slice through very easily. A dull blade or heavier knife will push the material apart and tend to tear at the surface. Use a steel or metal straightedge held firmly in place while making several light passes with the razor. Bearing down on the knife will only result in a sloppy cut or an injured finger. Thin stock up to about 3 plies can be cut with sharp scissors.

For outside curves, rough-cut the shape with several strokes of the razor, then finish with an emery board or sanding block (Fig. 6-6).

For inside curved sections, such as the arched top of interurban coach windows, cardstock may be finished with a simple sanding block. Rough-cut the opening with a razor leaving a little excess, then roll a piece of fine sandpaper around a dowel which is slightly smaller than the final opening. Sand to the finished size, then seal as needed.

Care should be taken to use a stiff cutting board below the Strathmore. Too soft a base will allow the cardstock to bend down along with the knife and form a creased edge. The cutting board should have no grain or the razor may wander off line following the wood grain.

Fig. 6-4. Sealed and painted cardstock can be made to look like metal, as in this simple oil drum.

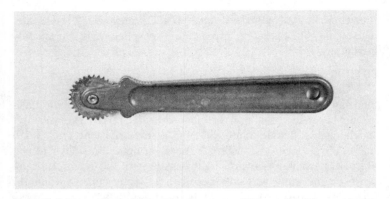

Fig. 6-5. A dressmaker's tracing wheel can be used to make rivet impressions in thin cardstock. With a metal ruler as a guide, uniform and evenly-spaced rivets can quickly be made.

GLUING

Many different types of glues will work with cardstock because it is porous. Water-based white glues like Elmer's should be avoided because warpage and ply separation will occur as the water is absorbed. A plastic cement like Testor's Acetate cement (model airplane glue) has only hydrocarbon solvents and will dry without warping the cardstock. Get a slower-setting cement that will absorb into the paper surface before beginning to "film over".

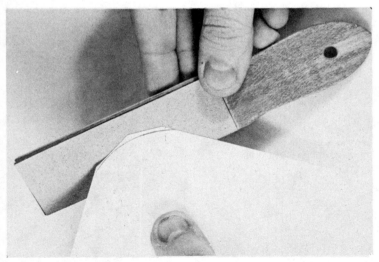

Fig. 6-6. Cardstock can be sanded to form rounded contours where a scissors or compass knife would be impractical.

110

Rough the surface with sandpaper, then squeeze out a generous line of cement on the pieces to be glued rather than trying to spread the cement, which will dry too fast. Cover the first piece with the laminate sheet and kind of smear this sandwich together, spreading the glue in-between. A little excess should ooze out of the seam to show full coverage. Place a piece of wood or particle board over the laminated sandwich to spread the force and press with several large weights for at least 30 minutes. This will give the glue solvents time to diffuse through the paper and assure a permanent bond.

Cardstock, like wood, has a grain. That is, it will flex more easily in one direction than in another. For greatest strength, the grains of the two pieces laminated should be at 90° or right angles to each other.

This lamination technique may be used to make economic poster board thickness by laminating a 1 or 2 ply Strathmore surface board to a less expensive cardboard back. Almost any thickness can be made by lamination.

Cardstock is a versatile and inexpensive material available in several formats. It is a good starting ground for developing your modeling skills. Let's go on now to some actual modeling projects that use cardstock as the basic modeling component.

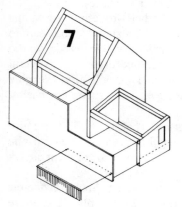

Building A Lineside Storage Shed

Whether at home or in business, the storage of miscellaneous materials can be a headache. You will need (or at least think you will need) the "stuff," but where to put it until then? Those cute little red barns or oversize dog houses are fine for the backyard, but industry's little odds and ends are frequently half-ton pieces of machinery, extra-wide wooden ties, barrels of spikes or nails. The list is varied and almost endless. To store these materials, lineside sheds of all types are built at strategic locations along the railroad. Frequently wooden, they are generally rather plain in design with large doors for easy access.

The prototype for this project is from the Quincy Mining Company in Hancock, Michigan (Figs. 7-1 through 7-6). Just a plain gray wooden structure, it will make an easy first project in working with paper. Located behind the main office building and adjacent to a stone machine shop, this little storage shed could handle anything from railroad supplies to old company files as the need would dictate. I don't have much in the way of particular details about its history and that's probably good since it represents the archetypal wooden structure that could just as easily be in Maine or Oregon. The rear wall is quite swayback and would represent a real challenge to the modeler. I've chosen to make the building in a slightly weathered but relatively new condition.

Begin by studying the scale plans (Figs. 7-7 through 7-9) and the photos of the prototype and model. Decide how you would begin construction. Would you use cast component windows or build them up individually?

Fig. 7-1. Quincy Mining Company prototype in Hancock, Michigan. From this view none of the foundation or footings show.

These are my kit-like instructions:

1. Select a high quality grade of paper stock. Paper comes in many forms including Bristol board, illustration board, museum

Fig. 7-2. Prototype—front view.

Fig. 7-3. The large double doors provide plenty of easy access for moving parts in and out.

board, and cardstock, among others. I prefer a hard, smooth-surfaced cardstock called Strathmore board. A small, embossed

Fig. 7-4. The swayback effect of the rear wall would offer some real modeling challenges.

thistle blossom in the corner is the symbol of the Strathmore company. The paper comes in one, two and three plies or thicknesses. I use the one and two ply stocks almost exclusively. For trim and overlays the one ply is excellent, while the two ply with a little bracing is fine for the body of the building. Many larger art supply stores carry cardstock. Avoid materials with mat or rough surfaces that will not stain properly. Also avoid stock that is

Fig. 7-5. Door details.

Fig. 7-6. Door details.

very thick. The thicker walls may need less bracing but will be frustrating to cut.

2. Tape your material to a flat surface and, with a ruler and small square, lay out the walls of your building in one piece. That is, draw a base line all the way from one end to the other and make all walls adjacent. The corners can be scored later and the basic box-like form of the structure made by folding the paper walls. Some people mark the windows and doors on the back side of the material to avoid having little overruns and smudges show on the finished wall. This requires a little extra thought though, since everything is backward. However, if you are careful, the drawing can be done directly on the face of the cardstock. If you are using cast windows, measure the back of the casting to determine the size hole needed to mount the window (Fig. 7-10).

3. The building exterior is made of 6″ boards, so with a good ruler mark off the boards along the wall or edge of each wall. Don't make marks in the middle of a wall which will show later. With your *dull* hobby knife and a metal ruler, scribe or score the board lines across each wall (Fig. 7-11). Don't try to scribe too long a section as the ruler may slip. Using a very sharp knife will slice a clean slit in the wall which, when later stained, may not show the gap between siding pieces. The dull knife should cut and form a sort of groove in the paper. Of course, too dull a knife will tear the paper,

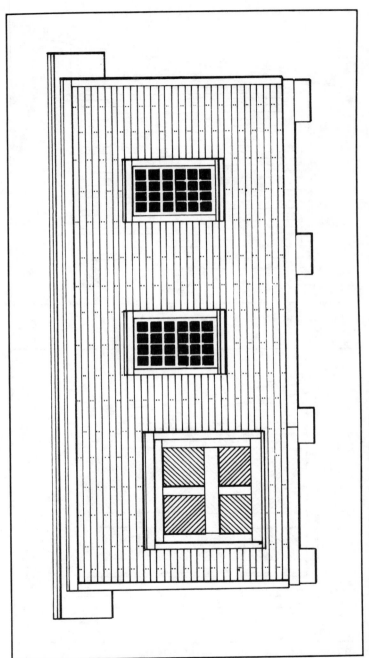

Fig. 7-7. Lineside storage shed—front view (HO scale).

117

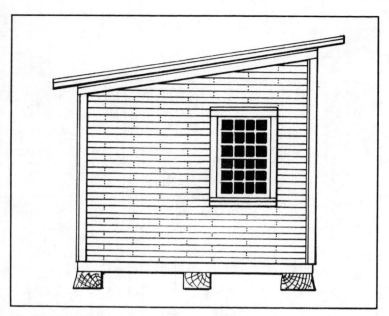

Fig. 7-8. Lineside storage shed—left side (HO scale).

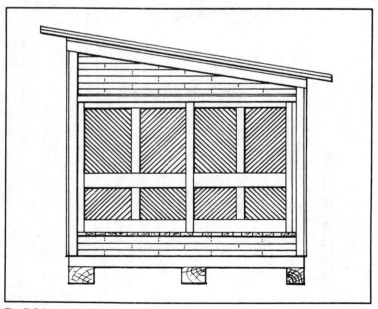

Fig. 7-9. Lineside storage shed—right side (HO scale).

118

Lineside Storage Shed	
Lumber Size	Scale Feet
1×6	500
1×10	350
1×3	160
2×10	50
1×2	50
2×6	150

3 Window castings
1 Large sheet 2 ply hard surface cardstock
  Miscellaneous scrap lumber for bracing (4×4's)
  Masking tape (about 3 scale feet wide)
  Gray stain, brown chalk or tempra powder
  White paint

Table 7-1. Bill of Materials.

so a little practice on a scrap piece of material is good. With a #16 or smaller X-acto knife blade, cut across a few of the boards at random to simulate the ends of short pieces of siding. With a longer blade, such as a #11, it is very easy to cut across two or more boards rather than just one. It may be a good idea to grind or file down one blade to *exactly* the width of a scale board so the cut can

Fig. 7-10. On a piece of good quality two-ply cardstock, lay out the structure from the plans. Make sure the openings for the windows are compatible with the casting you plan to use. *Don't* extend the lines any further than the actual openings or the pencil marks will show on the finished model.

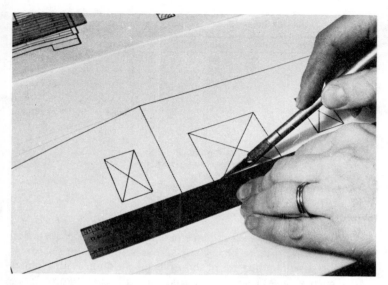

Fig. 7-11. With a dull knife and metal ruler, scribe lines for all the boards.

easily be made. Using the scriber (pin placed in the end of a dowel) and a square, push a number of nail holes into the siding. These will

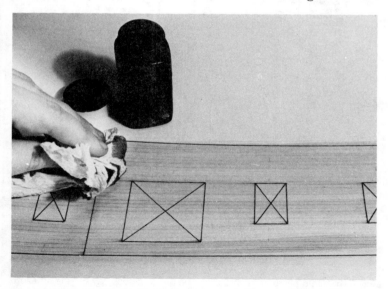

Fig. 7-12. Using a light black or gray wash and a paper towel pad, stain the building a light gray. Try not to be perfectly even and stain *only* in the direction of the boards, not across them.

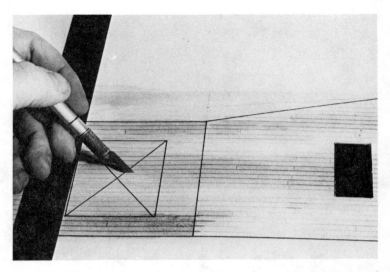

Fig. 7-13. With a very sharp knife cut out all the window and door openings and scribe (but don't cut through) the corners where the buildings will fold. Use the straight edge to protect the material you want to save in case the knife slips.

usually be placed in every other board down the wall in rows spaced at 16″ or 24″ centers.

4. Next, the walls are stained a very light gray. I use a mixture of black leather dye with rubbing alcohol. Very well thinned gray

Fig. 7-14. Place a second piece of cardstock behind the door openings and, with a sharp pencil, mark off the size of the door.

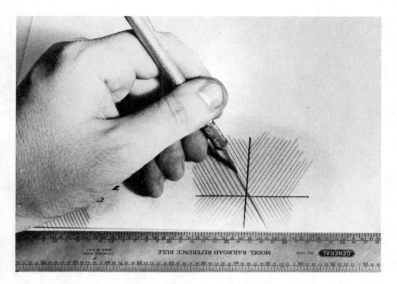

Fig. 7-15. Mark the centerlines for the door and scribe wood boards at 45° to the baseline. Be sure to extend the scribings well past the anticipated size of the door.

paint would be an alternative. Dab some of the stain on a pad and rub it briskly in the same direction as the siding. Try not to be perfectly uniform, but rather have some areas lighter or darker than others. After the stain has dried, use a small brush to apply

Fig. 7-16. With scrap lumber, build up a framing support behind the smaller door openings. This should be slightly thinner than the trim to be actually used for the doorway.

Fig. 7-17. Add the door framing first, then glue the scribed door to the back of the opening.

some additional stain to a board here or there to give a little variation to the walls. Notice how your scribing and nail holes will not turn much darker as they absorb the stain (Fig. 7-12).

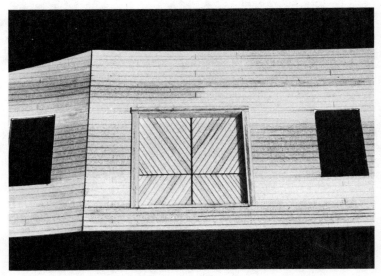

Fig. 7-18. Finish the door with the vertical edge pieces first, then add the horizontal top, middle, and bottom and finally the smaller vertical center pieces.

123

Fig. 7-19. The roof is a thick piece of cardboard, first darkened around the edges, then covered with layers of masking tape. Start at the bottom and work overlapping layers up to the top. Extra adhesive may be added to help the tape adhere.

5. Using a very sharp knife and ruler, cut out the window and door openings, being careful not to overrun into the main siding. Hold the ruler so that if the knife slips it will cut into the waste piece. Sharp scissors may be used for the long edges and bottom of the walls. Score but *do not* cut through the wall joints (Fig. 7-13).

6. Place a piece of new cardstock behind the door opening and with a very sharp pencil mark off the opening (Fig. 7-14). With a sharp pencil mark the vertical center line and the center of the horizontal trim piece. (Notice on the plans this is a little below the center.) With your dull knife and metal straight edge or drafting triangle, scribe the door boards at 45° according to the plans.

Fig. 7-20. The large opening for the double doors has been framed and many short pieces of 2x10's glued along the bottom for the heavy flooring.

Fig. 7-21. Additional cardstock was marked, then scribed for the double doors. Notice there are two separate doors that overlap.

Fig. 7-22. Vertical, then horizontal trim are added.

Scribe these right up to your center lines and *past* the marked edge of the door (Fig. 7-15). When the door is glued in place, your scribed boards will extend past the frame even if the positioning is not perfect.

Fig. 7-23. The finished doors are an interesting feature of the model.

Fig. 7-24. Window castings take most of the drudgery out of constructing the model.

7. Using scrap wood, glue a set of braces along the edges of the door openings. This should be a little thinner than the actual trim you plan to use for the framing. For example, I used 1x6'''s for

Fig. 7-25. The small patch on the roof breaks up the regular lines of the tar paper strips. More patches and even a hole or two would be appropriate, as the railroads ranked the lineside shed well down in maintenance priorities.

the door frame so 4x4's would be a good choice for the fillers (Fig. 7-16).

8. Prepaint all the wood trim flat white and stain with the gray wash. Use 1x6's to frame the two smaller door openings, doing the inside frame first and then the exterior. Finish the top of each door with a 1x2 rain cap piece (Fig. 7-17).

9. Apply a thin film of glue along the back of the door frame and set the scribed cardstock door in place. The frame should just cover your pencil marks. Build up the remainder of the doors with 1x6 and 1x10 prepainted and stained lumber. Cut and fit the long vertical pieces at the edges first. Add just a little glue and fit these tightly against the frame. Next come the horizontal pieces and finally the short center vertical ones (Fig. 7-18).

10. When the doors are dry, assemble the entire structure into a simple box, adding extra wooden bracing where necessary.

11. Using the model as a guide, cut out a thick piece of cardstock for a roof. There should be approximately a 1-foot overhang on all sides. On both sides paint the first inch or so back from the edge a dark black. Trim the edges of the roof with 2x6's. I used masking tape for the roofing, since it has a slightly rough surface that easily simulates old tar paper (Fig. 7-19). Make sure your tape is new and has plenty of adhesive. Some brands of masking tape have relatively low adhesion and will pull away in a few months. Frequently I will add a layer of contact or spray adhesive to the roof to hold the tape permanently in place. Paint the roof the flat or grimy black color of tar paper.

Fig. 7-26. The finished model, although primarily made of paper, has the look of weathered wood.

Fig. 7-27. Sawhorses, crates, and other accessories give the lineside shed a "lived in" look.

12. Turn the model over and glue it to the roof. There should be some additional bracing along the roof line of the model to act as a gluing surface for the roof.

13. Now add the 1x10 trim along the top of the walls along the roofline. Adding the trim at this time will hide any gaps or glue marks that may exist at the roof. Trim the corners with 1 x 3's.

14. The double set of large doors are assembled in the same fashion as the smaller doors with the exception that there are two overlapping paper bases. First, cut many short pieces of 2x10's and glue these at the bottom of the large door opening as flooring (Fig. 7-20). Try *not* to line them up perfectly, so the individual boards will show. Follow Figures 7-21 through 7-23 to finish the doors. The window castings may be glued in place at any time, just be sure that they are tightly held flush to the walls until the glue sets (Fig. 7-24).

15. Once the model is finished, a dusting of brown or gray chalk will age the roof (Fig. 7-25). Apply with a downward stroke and try to streak it a little bit. A gentle rubbing with a damp finger will remove excess chalk.

Finding a home for your model should be no problem at all, as every railroad needs someplace for that excess material. Be sure to surround your finished model with lots of scrap parts, junked pumps, machines and plenty of old boxes and crates (Fig. 7-26, 7-27).

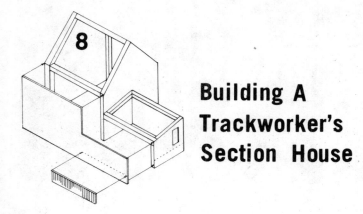

8

Building A
Trackworker's
Section House

Shelter is one of the basic elements of all our lives. In our modern existence we all seem to take a nice home or apartment as a guaranteed element of life. That, however, has not always been the case. Workers at the turn of the century experienced a wide range of housing styles that only in some cases were an improvement over the rowhouse sections of industrialized Europe. Many times the workers were simply dependent on the good intentions of the company to supply them with shelter. Among the most progressive was the Quincy Mining Company in Hancock, Michigan. Entire workers' towns were developed having a certain uniformity of style and design. For the miners' safety, telephones were installed in the mines before 1900. Reservoirs in the mines provided a water supply for the town below.

Similar types of buildings were used by the railroads to house workers during periods of heavy construction or repair. Transportation was not sufficiently developed to allow them to return to separate homes each day, so central section houses were used. This type of building could be found along almost any right-of-way, as miners' or loggers' shelters or as a private residence in one of the less affluent parts of town. The prototype for this structure was found above Hancock, Michigan in an area once known as Lower Pewaubic (Figs. 8-1 through 8-4). At one time there were blocks of identical, neat miners' houses that have long since been demolished. Only a few houses remain near the large brick and stone mine buildings. I suspect the additions and lean-to sort of sections have been added to a basic design. Feel free to modify as you wish.

Fig. 8-1. Our trackworkers' section house is modeled on this prototype in Hancock, Michigan.

The geographical heritage of the building is evident. The very steep roof pitch allows for high snow loads. In an area with 200-300 inches of snow annually, the sharp pitch is necessary. The small entry vestibule is a feature just being "discovered" again by energy designers but has been used for years where the winter wind routinely howls. The purpose is to prevent the cold wind from blowing directly into the house. A visitor must first enter the vestibule, close the door, then proceed on into the house.

Fig. 8-2. The steep roof, multiple chimneys, and entry vestiblule easily identify the structure as a north country home.

Trackworkers' Section House	
Size	Scale Feet
1×6	300
1×4	300
1×8	400

Scrap lumber for bracing
1 Large sheet 2-ply Strathmore board
1 Sheet heavy cardstock for roof
11 16-pane window castings
2 8-pane window castings
2 5-panel doors
2 Chimneys
Pins
Masking tape
Paints and Stains
Substitute for castings as desired

Table 8-1. Bill of Materials.

Two chimneys suggest there might be a parlor and kitchen stove used to heat the house. A nice pile of wood is neatly stacked outside the rear door.

Begin as usual by studying the plans (Figs. 8-5 through 8-8) and photos. The basic construction consists of one box for the main structure and two smaller boxes glued to it. I feel this is much easier than trying to glue together a multifolded pieces of cardstock.

Fig. 8-3. The house is a private residence that was once part of an entire company town known as Lower Pewaubic.

1. Begin by taping down a piece of 2-ply Strathmore board to your working surface. With a square and ruler, lay out the main portion of the structure using a sharp pencil. Try to make as few marks as possible. Use the actual window and door castings to establish the size of the openings. (See Chapter 7 for details.)

2. With a *dull* X-acto knife scribe the entire structure. Go well beyond the edges of the building. With a pad of cotton or gauze, smear a light coloring of light red and brown over the building. Try *not* to be uniform and vary the tone. After the paint is dry, finish the walls with a rubbing of very light gray or black stain as described in Chapter 7.

3. Using a very sharp knife or scissors cut out the openings.

4. Using scrap lumber, add bracing to the bottom, top and corners of the building. These need only be flush with the edge of the wall at the top where they will form the gluing surface for the roof. Be sure to use only a film of glue and clamp them in place with clothespins while drying. Small cardstock triangles or cross braces may be added across the corners for extra stability.

5. Apply a little plastic cement and glue each window into place and allow to dry. Assemble the entire structure into a box form. Use a large square to assure the perpendicular corners of the box (Fig. 8-9).

6. From thick cardstock (I use 1/16″ illustration board for my O scale models), cut the roof sections. Measure these directly from

Fig. 8-4. Right side of the trackworkers' section house.

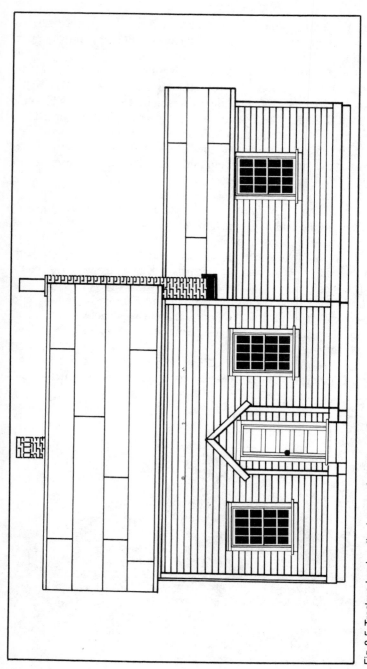

Fig. 8-5. Trackworkers' section house—front view (HO scale).

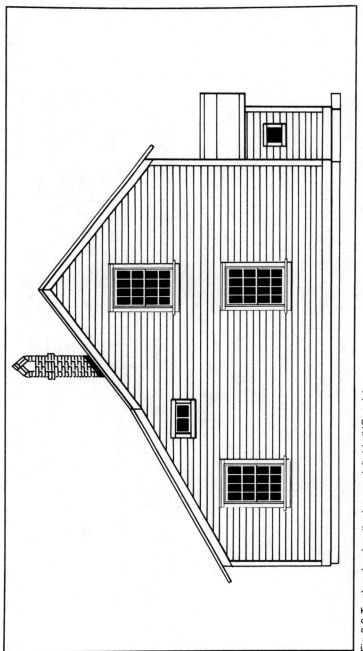

Fig. 8-6. Trackworkers' section house—left side (HO scale).

135

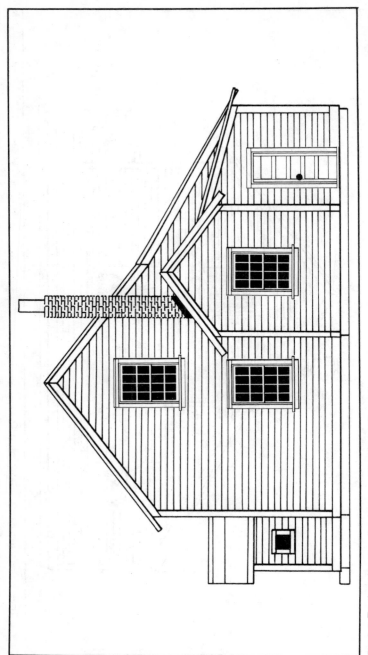

Fig. 8-7. Trackworkers' section house—right side (HO scale).

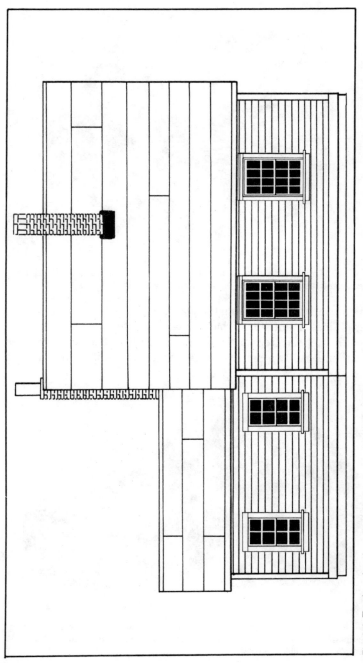

Fig. 8-8. Trackworkers' section house—back view (HO scale).

Fig. 8-9. The basic model is made from cardstock, scribed and stained a weathered red or brown color. Notice the sturdy bracing inside the shell.

the model rather than from the plans. Use about a 1-foot overhang on all sides. Paint the overhang black or dark brown.

7. Repeat steps 1-6 for the vestibule and side room. The vestibule has two small windows that were built up from short pieces of strip wood (Fig. 8-10).

Fig. 8-10. The building is actually made from three separate box-like subassemblies. It seemed easier to use three smaller boxes rather than one complicated multifolded piece.

Fig. 8-11. The roof is a piece of thick cardstock with extra adhesive and strips of masking tape to represent roofing paper. The tape is allowed to extend past the edge of the roof, then is cut back with a sharp knife. Grimy black paint covers the roof.

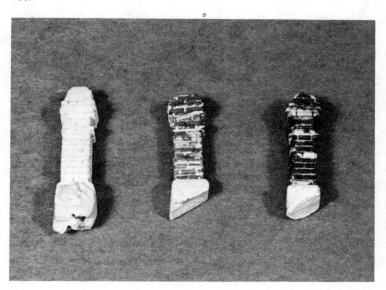

Fig. 8-12. Castings were used for the chimneys. At the left is the raw casting which is painted completely white. Red and yellow paint are applied to the face of the bricks only (center); finally the entire chimney is washed with a black or gray stain to blend the colors and show weathering.

Fig. 8-13. The tall chimney for the sidebuilding is actually pieces of three chimney castings—one bottom, one middle, and one for the top. Commercial castings of chimneys are also readily available.

8. Glue together the three box-like subassemblies and add the 1 x 8 trim along the top and bottom of each wall with 1 x 4 corner trim. Finish the roof with an edging of 1 x 6.

9. Coat the roof with spray adhesive or rubber type cement. Cover the roof with thin strips of masking tape (about 3 scale feet wide), working from the bottom up and overlapping a little less

Fig. 8-14. Once the roof is completed (left) it is dusted with powdered brown chalk or tempra color (center). Finally the excess dust powder is blown away and the roof wiped with a moist finger until the texture of the tape is evident (right).

Fig. 8-15. The vestibule has small windows made of just a few bits of 1 x 6 trim. The door is a commercial casting with a small pin painted white as a door knob.

Fig. 8-16. Our finished model well captures the look and feel of the prototype structure.

than 1 foot. Press this down firmly for good adhesion. I ran the tape over the edge of the roof, then cut it back to the exact edge of the gable. Add a patch here or there and paint the entire roof grimy black (Fig. 8-11).

Fig. 8-17. Note the authentic look of the "tar paper" roof.

Fig. 8-18. The trackworkers' section house will add to any model train layout.

10. Cut the roof back where the chimney from the kitchen extends above the roof. I used the castings from Chapter 13 by cutting down the smaller chimneys and piecing them together to make one large one (Fig. 8-12, 8-13). If you are not interested in casting at this time, a simple chimney can be made by wrapping a piece of wood stock with paper printed with a colored brick pattern, or a plastic sheet that has embossed bricks. A third alternative is to actually saw-cut the bricks into a piece of wood or plaster. This is very tedious and usually is reserved for making very special patterns for casting in plaster. Several manufacturers also make very nice castings of chimneys at a nominal cost. Get to know your local hobby shop dealer, as he can direct you to the best source of castings. Paint the chimney white first, then paint the tops of the bricks red with an occasional yellow one. Finally, wash the chimneys with a black stain. Cut the bottom of the casting to the roof contour and glue in place.

11. Dust the roof with a healthy application of powdered brown chalk or tempra colors. Work this down the roof. Blow off the excess, wet your fingers with a little water, and wipe off the dust until the textured surface of the masking tape is evident (Fig. 8-14). Again, don't be uniform, but make some areas lighter and others darker. A little dark wash at the base of the chimneys should be heavy near the chimney and thin out down the roof.

12. Position the building on your layout near the tracks and begin moving in the crews and track workers (Figs. 8-15 through 8-18). If you're really pleased with your efforts perhaps you might want to build a whole workers' town!

Chicago and Northwestern freighthouse model constructed of wood, cardstock, plaster, and plastic castings.

Chicago and Northwestern drainage bridge. Construction details are in Chapter 4.

The advertising (press-type lettering) adds interest to the Schultz' Brothers icehouse. Construction details are in Chapter 5.

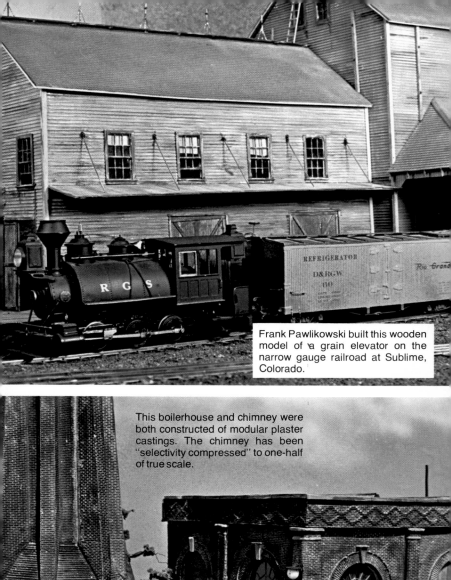

Frank Pawlikowski built this wooden model of a grain elevator on the narrow gauge railroad at Sublime, Colorado.

This boilerhouse and chimney were both constructed of modular plaster castings. The chimney has been "selectivity compressed" to one-half of true scale.

A ... de ...l ..ll.d f.... ...ndst...e so the Chicago Burlington and Quincy. This model is made from modular plaster castings.

Front view of foundry. Chimneys are made from ¾″ plastic water pipe.

Back view of foundry. Even the window frames and muntins are made of plaster castings.

The foundry makes an impressive addition to the model railroad layout.

Detail view of foundry. Roof is made of masking tape.

This machine shop is constructed of Vollmar plastic stone, with window details from plaster castings.

The machine shop features a "corrugated tin" roof made by forming aluminum foil over scribed wood sheeting stock.

A lineside shed and watchman's shanty constructed of wood. A shed of this sort would have been used for handcar storage.

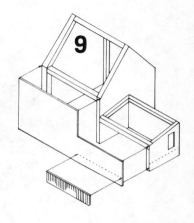

Working with Plaster

9

When you discuss modeling materials, conversations usually center around the more conventional media such as wood, plastic, and brass. There is, however, a growing interest in ordinary plaster as an effective and easy-to-use medium. For years plaster has been used in industry for design work because of its ease in handling and ability to form smooth, even curves. With the rising cost of all modeling materials, plaster offers the additional advantage to the modeler of being one of the least expensive.

The prime mover in the introduction of plaster to the modeler has been the development of several soft rubber molding compounds usually called silicone or RTV (room temperature vulcanizing) rubbers. In industrial size quantities, these materials are available from the major suppliers such as Dow and General Electric. Smaller speciality houses such as the Castolite Company make these materials available to the hobbyist. There is no real benefit to getting two or three gallons from Dow since the shelf or storage life of the rubber is limited to 9-12 months at the most if sealed and less once opened. The biggest improvement in rubber is the development of highly fluid, easy-pour rubbers like Castolite SR-P. This material pours like milk and requires no special tools to make excellent molds. Carving an entire model out of a hunk of plaster offers no real advantage over conventional modeling methods. Where plaster modeling excels is the simulation of structures having some regular and repeating structural pattern; that is, one section of wall or other architectural features repeat in the model. For example, the boilerhouse in Fig. 9-1 has a modular wall section—one window and the associated pilaster (vertical

Fig. 9-1. Modular construction made both the large boilerhouse and the chimney possible. Each window section was cast separately, then joined together to make the final structure. The door section is also the same casting with the door opening made by enlarging the window area.

brick pillar) which are actually cast separately, then ganged together to make the finished model (Fig. 9-2). The model can be completed in only a fraction of the time that would be needed if each section was built up individually.

Plaster is, of course, best suited to simulate stone and brick buildings. Concrete castings, window sills, foundations, and footings are also easy to make and reduce in plaster (Figs. 9-3, 9-4).

Taking things one step further, kit manufacturer Tom Yorke offered several wooden prototypes actually made from plaster. Knotholes, nailmarks, and cracked boards may easily be simulated. Although it is hard to stain the plaster "wood" to look like raw lumber, a painted and weathered wooden structure is easy to do. The Chicago Burlington and Quincy brass foundry (Figs. 9-5, 9-6) is all cast plaster including the windows, muntins, and frames. Notice how the window sections repeat down the side.

Fig. 9-2. By making a pattern for only part of the building, then putting the castings together, a building of any dimension can be made.

Plaster may also be used to copy small parts such as the passenger car furniture in Fig. 9-7. The original pattern may easily

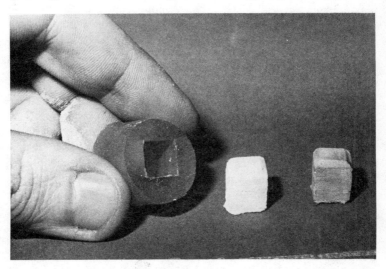

Fig. 9-3. At the left is a soft rubber mold for a small concrete pier or footing. In the center is the raw plaster casting. The finished pier is on the right. Even the grain of the wooden frame shows in the finished casting. For a coaling tower or water tank, you may need ten or twenty of these piers. Isn't it nice to be able to cast them rather than carve each one separately?

Fig. 9-4. The curved window lintels (top frame) were made by carving one original from wood, then casting the rest in plaster. This building required ten of the lintels. The window sills are also special castings made in the same fashion.

be reproduced 100 or more times. Compared to wood or metal, plaster may be carved, shaved, filed, chipped, and ground with only the simplest hand tools. Some caution must be exercised, as a slip of the hand can remove several scale inches. But considering the cost of the material, the loss of a few castings is generally quite acceptable. Hand carving need not be only for the Michaelangelos. The chimney for a Chicago and Northwestern freighthouse (Fig. 9-8) was carved from plaster with an ordinary hobby knife. The secret is that there are actually six small squares of plaster. Each one was carved to the correct contour, then stacked to make the chimney. The top was finished with files for the square shape. Being no sculptor, I'm not ashamed to say I threw away three pieces for every one I used. By using the stacking method, however, the entire chimney was not sacrificed for one mistake.

The quarried stone foundation of the same freighthouse (Fig. 9-9) was made with an even easier method that I call my "broken sheet" method. The rough texture of the stone is achieved by pouring a sheet of plaster approximately 1 scale foot deep and allowing this to dry. The sheet is scored with a knife into 3′ wide sections which are broken off in long strips. The rough edges of the sheets are scored again with a knife at about 2-3′ intervals and then stacked with their edges showing outward and the scored blocks

Fig. 9-5. This wooden foundry on the Chicago Burlington and Quincy is completely made from plaster castings, including the windows. The long wall is actually a repeating pattern of sets of double windows. These were cast separately and joined together to make the wall. The large walls are cast from plaster, with holes cut and various window pieces glued in place. The entire structure is filled with a sealer, then painted white, and finally washed with a gray stain.

Fig. 9-6. Because the plaster can be easily carved and cut, it's easy to add details. The large rooftop ventilators were made from wood, and the roof is a large sheet of illustration board.

alternating. The effect is an instant stone block wall with almost no fuss. The wall can be sprayed to simulate granite or sandstone and finished with a dusting of black chalk dust to highlight the textured

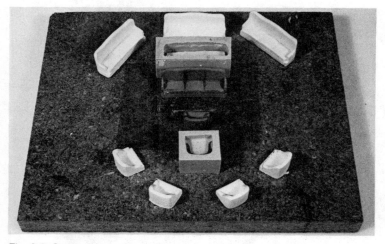

Fig. 9-7. Small pieces of furniture were needed for a model railroad car. The original patterns are in the middle of the photo, surrounded by the molds, and a few of the white plaster castings. These will be used in an American Standard Car Company O scale passenger car.

158

surface. Plaster is a most versatile material. Some day I'll try an entire stone building in broken plaster.

Many rural buildings are made with rough fieldstone foundations—random-shaped rocks held together with cement or mortar. For a miner's house foundation (Fig. 9-10), I tried and failed to make a real scale two foot thick wall. The foundation kept cracking and I could not seem to get enough stones into the plaster. Instead I went to a solid pad foundation extending all the way across the building. If you're not modeling the interior of the basement, no one will ever see the extra plaster. I made a frame the size of the entire foundation and filled it with a fine stone gravel. Depending on your scale, anything from fishbowl gravel to small road stone can be used. A light mix of plaster was poured over it and a piece of glass placed over the top to level the mix. Once the pad had set, the frame was removed and while still wet a stiff wire brush was used to scrub away most of the surface plaster and expose the stone (Fig. 9-11). A washing with a gray or black stain will dull the white plaster color.

I'm sure many more creative ways of using plaster will be developed by modelers. In general, it is a new area in which we can all experiment with surprisingly interesting results.

Fig. 9-8. Plaster can be carved to form very useful models, whether for a single item (this old time chimney), or a pattern master. This chimney was carved in seven sections from the base up. Trying to carve the chimney from a single piece of plaster proved impossible, but with the subassembly method, each piece could be examined. Several were made and the best were accepted.

Fig. 9-9. Broken strips of plaster were used to make the foundation for this structure. A light dusting of charcoal powder highlights the rough texture of the plaster wall.

REASONS FOR CASTING

Why study the casting process? The commercial market already provides a wide range of castings for many common prototypes; why bother with your own castings? With the cost of materials and my time, I would never copy a commercial casting. However, *common* is the key word. For a *special* model we need a particular casting that may be identical to the prototype or at least capture its flavor. The commercial supplier must aim for the major market with the widest appeal. For that special model in my own collection, I'm willing to invest the extra time and effort to have exactly the right part.

With the larger models it's a matter of time and money. Without casting, some projects would simply never have been done. I started my Chicago, Burlington and Quincy brass foundary project in 1965. It promptly never got past the scale drawing stage. I just couldn't bring myself to cutting out the wood to make all those windows. Then the idea of casting it in repeating modules came along, and in less than three months of odd evenings it was done. By breaking down the design into a series of repeating modules, the project became exciting and rather easy to do. The pleasure of lifting a new finished casting from its mold can be almost

Fig. 9-10. A fieldstone foundation is found in many rural areas of the country. The stones in this case are a smooth form of gravel called "pea" gravel which might be a little big for the smaller scales. Look around for different types of materials that will fit your modeling needs.

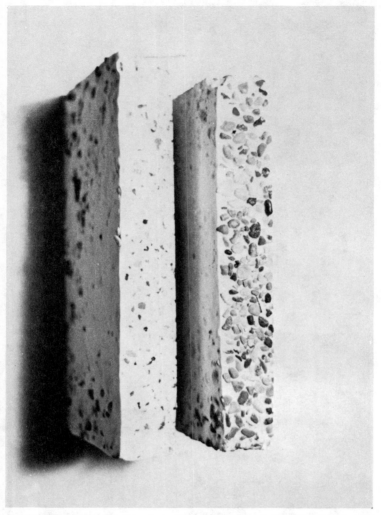

Fig. 9-11. The left pad is a rough casting removed from the mold while still moist. At the right, a still brush has been used to scrap away the excess plaster and expose the small stones.

intoxicating. I call it molder's disease—you just want to make one more casting, then one more, then one more.....

In addition, the costs of some modeling supplies are just going out of sight. The raw materials may be hard to come by and the labor needed to finish the piece just very expensive. No one makes a brick faced module like those in my Milwaukee Road boilerhouse, yet there is over $3.00 worth of plastic brick material alone in the section. At that rate the entire structure would have taken over $45.00 in brick stock. I could afford neither the time nor the cost of the material for that building. However, less than $3.00 worth of plaster was used to make the *entire* building. Casting was a great economy both in time and materials.

Is it expensive? If you've been following the other sections of this book and have acquired the basic modelers tools indicated, you will only need to purchase the molding rubbers and plaster to get started.

Can you expect good results the first few times? Absolutely! If you start with the simple projects described here, especially a flat-faced mold, you should be able to make a near perfect mold on the first try. Once, after pouring a mold for another project, I had a little Castimold SR-P left over and I didn't know what to do with it. I casually just glopped the rubber onto a sheet of plastic brick paper on the bench. The next day I had a perfect mold of the embossed brick face, without a single bubble and with every detail...no dikes, no fancy equipment, no trouble. For a copy mold, I'd be a little more careful and design my mold with more realism, but the basic principles are incredibly simple. Make a pattern, build a dike around the pattern, mix the rubbers according to directions, pour very slowly to minimize bubbles, let dry overnight, and then carefully remove your mold.

How long does casting take? Casting may require you to harness your production line training and move back to a slower time. Patterns are no different than any other modeling project, so the time spent will depend on your normal modeling skills. The molding rubbers cure in about 12 to 24 hours. I normally save the pouring of the rubber for the last project in the evening so I can leave it overnight and remove the mold when I return home from work. Normal plaster castings take about 20 minutes to set up and, depending on how elaborate they are, a longer drying time may be required. Popping them out too soon may crack a weak casting. Waiting too long sometimes causes the part to stick a bit which also may cause cracking. For the modular type buildings, I will normally make four or five castings per day, allowing each to set up well before removing it from the mold.

If I've convinced you that casting really is a skill you would like to add to your modeling repertoire, let's move on to the elements of patterns and mold making, and then to a few sample projects.

PLASTER—MORE THAN A WALL COVERING

Plaster, as with many building materials, has its origins in nature. As gypsum, a rock-like mineral, it was used in Roman times as a construction material although simple lime was more common. Lime is an alkaline, very slow setting material when used as mortar, although extremely durable, hardening over the centuries to a very tough substance. Unfortunately, its alkaline nature makes it very susceptible to the modern phenomena of air pollution where acid-type gases cause rapid and irreversible damage. Rapid-setting plasters have now almost completely replaced lime as a construction material.

Browsing through the catalogs of various material suppliers will show ten or more different types of plasters for construction purposes. For modeling we will limit ourselves to only two of the most common types.

Plaster is made by taking the chemical gypsum (calcium sulfate in a crystal form with two molecules of water) and heating the solid to remove part or all of the water. The finished pebbles are ground to a fine powder and packaged for use. In the hardware store you will probably find plaster-of-paris, patching plaster, or perhaps molding plaster. These are all partially hydrated plasters from which only part of the water has been removed. When the powder is mixed with water, the original mineral begins to grow and sets to a solid mass. This is actually a chemical reaction from which you can feel the heat released. Both the Romans and ancient Egyptians knew of and used plasters. However, gypsum sets very rapidly (5-20 minutes), and until modern retarding agents were discovered, plaster was a poor building material. For model work, a few drops of ordinary vinegar will slow the setting process.

Another interesting feature of plaster as a molding agent is that it expands slightly in curing so it will push into the corners, cracks and crevices of your mold, capturing every detail. The expansion is slight, up to 0.4%, but is important. Some special plasters like high expansion Hydrocal Cement are specifically designed for extreme expansion in certain industrial molding processes.

The general characteristics of the partially or "hemihydrated" plasters are that they set relatively quickly, and are light and quite soft. The surface is easily carved and the parts break easily. Of course, the strength of the casting also depends on the amount of water added. The more water over the optimum amount, the weaker the castings and the longer the setting times. Too *little* water causes instant setting, flaking and very poor pouring characteristics. As an inexpensive way to get started in plaster casting, plaster of Paris is fine.

Most hardwall plasters (construction plasters) have some clay or other chemical mixed with it to retard setting. The times can range up to 2-4 hours. For making a few small castings, this time delay is unnecessary and inconvenient. "Gauging" plasters have lime added for plasticity and workability, while "lightweight" plasters incorporate fillers like vermiculite to lower the density. These are specialized building materials that you are not likely to find in the hardware store and they are not suggested. I mention them just because the word "plaster" covers a range of materials and there are many brands, variations and uses. Pick one type and develop your own skills with that material.

The second class of plasters are those where the heating of the pure gypsum drives off all the water, giving an anhydrous or waterless form. When water is added to these powders a different behavior is seen. Setting times are very long and expansion is less but the finished molding is very hard, in some cases almost stonelike. These materials are generally classed as *Keene's cements* and have various materials added to speed the setting process. Without accelerators, setting times of 6-12 hours are possible. In small molds with the correct water mix and appropriate accelerators, setting times of 20 minutes are more common. Commercially these materials are available under the names Hydrocal, Ultracal, Hydro-stone, and Craftstone, among others. These materials are generally available only in large quantities to the building trade. Many craft shops and mail order firms like Castolite offer them in smaller quantities for the modeler. There is no real savings in buying a 100 pound bag if you intend to do only small castings on an occasional basis. Because these are the waterless type powders they tend to pick up moisture from the air and lose some of their reactive properties. The manufacturers suggest storage for only 90 days to maintain optimum strength, but I've kept small bags double wrapped in plastic for years without noticeable changes in setting time. Really, what's a few minutes in making some small parts? I did once buy a big bag of molding plaster and kept it in the garage over the winter only to find a 50 pound solid lump in the spring.

For castings with very thin sections which may be subjected to some stress, the hard hydrocal type plasters are very good. If you plan to do fine detail carving rather than massive removal of

Fig. 9-12. The tough nature of Hydrocal was used to allow the carving of the round window in the wall peak. A thin sheet of well-dried Craftstone was carved with an ordinary compass to make the round window.

material, the harder castings are best (Figs. 9-12, 9-13). Soft patching plaster parts tend to break and shatter when carved. I've cast entire buildings from Craftstone (Castolite Company) with walls only 1/16" thick with no difficulty. Some plasters are diluted

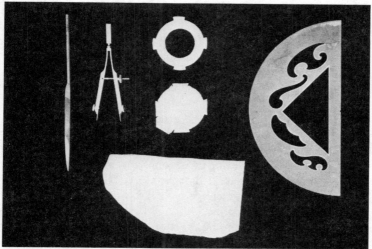

Fig. 9-13. The muntins are small pieces of wood.

166

with powders such as fillers, binders and extenders to change their setting or surface characteristics. Beware of those materials containing asbestos fibers which, when inhaled, pose a serious health problem. Without proper breathing masks and ventilation, I would prefer plasters (such as Craftstone-FR) which contain small plastic or fiberglass pieces to increase bonding power and strength.

I don't feel it's necessary for the modeler to study all the details of the many different kinds of plasters. Rather, become familiar with one of the lighter plasters from the local hardware stores; also stock up on one brand of the harder types from a craft or hobby shop. Your experience will be more important than twenty different data sheets from one of the manufacturers. Because it is porous, plaster may easily be glued with white glues such as Elmer's or Ambroid.

Plaster is a versatile and useful modeling material that, with a little practice, can significantly widen the skills of any hobbyist.

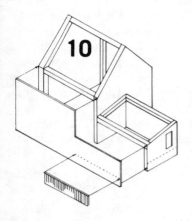

10

Plaster
Pattern Making

My first thought is to remind you that from one master you can easily make one hundred copies, yet each copy can be no better than your original. Remember that every error, imperfection, or rough surface will be clearly and permanently reproduced. Decide when you start to make the master as perfect as possible. Throw away those pieces that don't meet your maximum standards. Doing a part over three or four times is not a condemnation of your skills, but rather a tribute to your sense of excellence. Of course, you never will make the perfect master but we all must push ourselves to do just a little bit better job each time.

Because the liquid rubbers are virtually nonreactive to other substances and the setting process takes place at room temperature, almost any materials may be used for making the patterns. Wood, cardstock, metal, plastic and even plaster itself may be used in any combination and proportion. There is no problem in using any or all of these materials in the same pattern. Wood, of course, simulates wood very easily, while I like to use plastic to represent metal because of its ease in handling, cutting, and gluing. (The truth is I cannot solder worth a darn.) When shapes need to be carved, I prefer plaster itself as the pattern. For large pieces use a soft plaster such as plaster of Paris, while for small and crisp patterns the harder Hydrocal or Craftstone plasters would be best. If a piece needs to be turned or drilled, then metal is a good choice as plaster will easily crack. Long straight pieces are best made with strip wood or strips of styrene available at your hobby shop. Wood should be sealed with a filler or sanding sealer to prevent the rubber from creeping into the end grain. Once the rubber has entered the wood it is very hard to remove the mold from the pattern and may cause tears. I would not suggest using balsa wood as a pattern material unless it is extremely well sealed because of the very course balsa grain.

Sometimes a mold seems to just pop off the pattern, while other times it holds on very tightly. If the pattern is very large a slight *draft angle* will allow easy release (Fig. 10-1). For most model applications this is not necessary, although it is common practice in industrial work. The problem generally involves an undercut or *key lock* in the patttern. Because the silicone rubbers are very flexible, it's possible to allow the rubber to actually slide underneath projections of the patterns. The mold must be partially distended in one direction to release the undercut, then remove the part. There is a limit to the stretching ability of the mold, so limit undercuts as much as possible. Be prepared for a number of broken

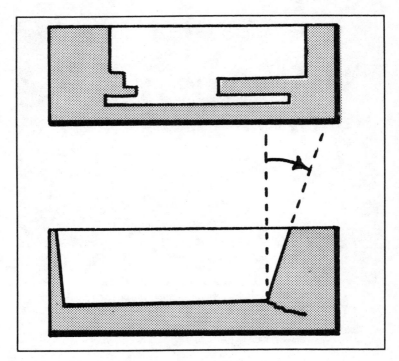

Fig. 10-1. Draft angle and undercuts (not to scale).

Fig. 10-2. The concrete cornice of an older commercial building would make an easy one-sided pattern. It could be used to dress up a simple kit structure, or to detail a completely scratchbuilt one. Notice the symmetry directly through the middle of the window. Each half reflects the other like a mirror. Your eye will quickly detect an error if one side is not the reflection of the other. It is better to be symmetrical than to copy the prototype exactly; that is, a lopsided window looks bad, but if the pattern is a little too long on *both* sides no one will notice.

castings since there may be a definite sequence of pulls, tugs and twists before the mold will properly release. In one of my early patterns I completely ignored an undercut problem and simply couldn't remove the mold at all. I learned a lot from that experience.

SYMMETRY OF DESIGN

Having selected the pattern materials, a good deal of thinking should go into your pattern design before even reaching for your X-acto knives. We want a pattern that looks perfect even if it may have a defect or two. I begin by looking for the symmetry of the

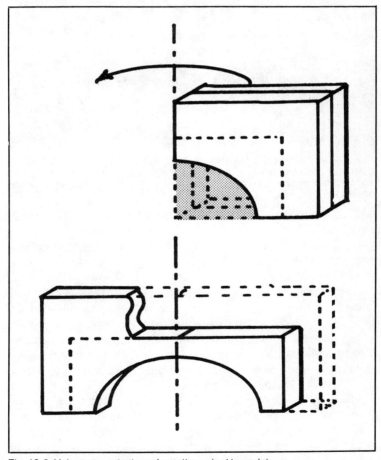

Fig. 10-3. Using symmetry to make patterns (not to scale).

Fig. 10-4. The symmetry of this concrete highway bridge can be used to limit the number of castings needed to make the model. Each side is actually split in half and each of these halves is actually the same casting just turned around where necessary.

design. Nature has an abundance of symmetry, starting with molecular patterns and extending all the way to the galaxies.

For example, consider a rounded window arch casting in a commercial building (Fig. 10-2). Depending on your skills you may be able to cut a very smooth curve on each side of the arch. However, unless both sides of the arch are identical, your eye will immediately catch the error. If both curves are the same whether or not they match the prototype, your pattern will be completely acceptable. Look for the mirror or reflection planes in a pattern, then build the pattern to have identical sides. Again, my philosophy is to make the pattern *look* acceptable rather than attempting perfection and having it look bad. A simple way to make the arch is to glue two pieces of wood or plastic together (at the ends only), then carve or cut one side of the arch. Separate the two pieces, turn one over, and match the two pieces to make the arch (Fig. 10-3). Your eye will view both sides of the arch as identical and not really detect if the curvature or length are not exactly perfect.

When studying the symmetry of a piece, you may discover you need not cast all of the object. Only a part may be necessary, which can be repositioned to complete the model. Only one quarter of the highway bridge (Fig. 10-4) need be cast. The finished castings (Fig. 10-5) may be turned around and placed in sets of four to make the finished bridge.

For some types of patterns it may be useful to make a casting of one part, make multiple copies and use the copies in a more complex pattern. For example, a very ornate concrete bridge spans the Kishwaukee River in Belvidere, Illinois (Fig. 10-6). It would be very nice to cast this bridge in sections each having ten of the sculptured balusters (posts) with the top and bottom railings in place. Each of the posts must be identical and there is no way I could carve ten identical posts. Instead I would make only *one* baluster as perfectly as possible, make a mold of it and cast ten to twelve copies. The best of these would be used in making the next pattern to finish the sectional bridge mold. This type of concrete railing could also be used for public buildings, railroad stations, sports stadia and similarly detailed buildings.

CASTING STRUCTURES

A multitude of structures do not lend themselves to wood or paper construction. These are generally stone or brick that are of a later vintage and tend to be well preserved even today. There are several ways to represent these materials, including plastic

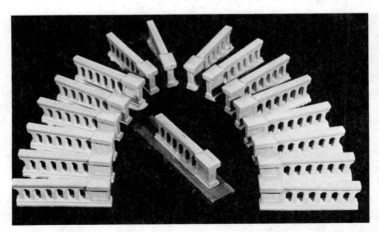

Fig. 10-5. The pattern in the center is surrounded by copies that may be used to make a bridge or a station wall.

173

Fig. 10-6. Crossing the Kishwaukee River, this rather ornate bridge is dedicated to the veterans of American wars overseas. Note that the bridge is again a series of repeating modules, each containing 10 curved posts. It would be impossible for me to carve ten identical posts. Rather, I would make one as best I could, then make a mold and copy it 10 or 15 times, take the 10 best of these and use them to make a second pattern for just one part of the bridge. Copies of *that* pattern would then make the final bridge.

imitation brick paper sheets and printed brick paper. These materials can be very useful for a small brick or stone structure, but many of the buildings important enough to be built in brick were rather large and might have dozens, even hundreds of windows, doors, bays etc. These are an overwhelming challenge to even the most dedicated of modelers.

But don't give up hope. If the prototype has a repetitive pattern it can easily be cast from one module and even very large models can be made from the one pattern. A good example of this type of building is the boilerhouse in Fig. 10-7 which could be made from a single pattern and multiple plaster castings glued together. It could be modified with large doors at the ends to make a repair shop or interurban car shed. The warehouse in Fig. 10-8 is located in Belvidere, Illinois and has a very simple box-like design. Because the back is really not much more interesting than the front, this prototype would make an excellent backdrop model with only one wall extending just a few scale feet to the tracks. The impression of a large building is given while only using a small fraction of the available space. For this type of structure, casting

Fig. 10-7. Each window section makes a simple repeating module for this boilerhouse in Milwaukee, Wisconsin.

Fig. 10-8. This rather plain furniture warehouse in Belvidere, Illinois would make an excellent background model only 8 or 10 scale feet deep. Propped up against the wall, it would look like a huge building but only take a few inches of layout space.

might be done in epoxy or very hard plasters since a tall thin casting is necessary. The Chicago and Northwestern freighthouse located in Rockford, Illinois (Figs. 10-9, 10-10) might make a good addition to a small pike's terminal city or to a big city freight-handling terminal. Again it has a repeat pattern that can be modeled in a single unit then repeated over and over again. The office area at one end is different, but with just a little extra modeling it is possible to generate a distinctive and most interesting building.

This is not the limit of plaster casting techniques. Many small structures are cast entirely from concrete, including sign posts and signal boxes. Believe it or not, some gondola cars during war-time metal shortages were actually cast from concrete. With the ever-increasing cost of wood and the availability of modeling time, some modelers and manufacturers have taken to modeling wooden structures and copying the basic pattern in plaster.

The same concept holds if a repeating pattern can be discerned in the prototype. Then one master pattern can be made, a mold prepared, and multiple copies produced. Plaster is a marvelous material that can easily reproduce the grain and texture of even the finest wood detail. Finishing is a critical factor to make a credible model. We will consider several different types of

Fig. 10-9. Again the repeating nature of factory building design can be seen in this Chicago and Northwestern freighthouse in Rockford, Illinois. Each receiving dock could be a separate module, cast and simply glued together to make the final model.

Fig. 10-10. The office area is unique with a distinctive railroad herald painted on the brickwork. Most of this part might have to be built separately, but would provide a nice diversion from the regularity of the cast part.

projects so that you can start with the simplest or a more complicated project.

PICKING THE PROTOTYPE AND SELECTIVE COMPRESSION

In almost any modeling scale, many prototype structures tend to be of enormous proportions. The Pennsylvania Railroad Shops

Fig. 10-11. The parting lines for the east wall are hidden behind the pilasters (vertical posts). The posts could also be cast separately, then glued over the joints in the wall castings behind them.

178

at Altoona were a city unto themselves. Structures *hundreds* of feet long were not unusual. Modeling these even in the smallest scales would probably be impractical. Cutting a thousand or so holes for windows is an unappetizing task.

However, it is still entirely possible to capture the *feeling* and *atmosphere* without the bulk. This is called *selective compression*. The modeler seeks out the important and distinctive features of the prototype and includes these in his model, while generally reducing the overall dimensions of the building. For example, the Rockford freighthouse over 700 feet long. That's 175 inches or 14.6 feet if modeled on O scale. An equally distinctive model could be by reducing the length to 175 feet, dropping the number of doors to 5, and shrinking the building. The distinctive stone office area would be retained almost intact leaving room for the railroad herald on the upper wall.

PARTING LINES

In designing your pattern, you must also look ahead to both the molding process and how the finished castings will be used. For the molding process we want the *parting line*, or place where the mold

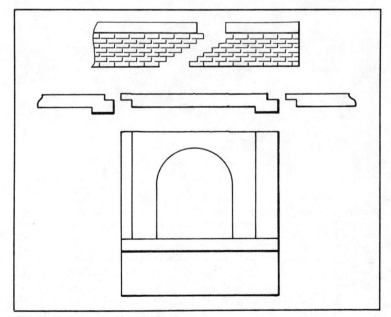

Fig. 10-12. Parting lines (not to scale).

Fig. 10-13. Eight separate castings make up this ornate chimney. It was designed by Erasmus Levitt for the Calumet Mining Company in Calumet, Michigan before the turn of the century. The model is compressed to only half of its actual size. A model truly reduced to scale would dwarf the entire modeling scene. The finished casting weighs more than 10 pounds.

halves join, to be as inconspicuous as possible. For the finished castings it is important that consideration be given to how these pieces will join and how the gaps or junctions will be disguised.

Examine almost any commercial casting and you will find a line or place where the two halves of the mold joined. Depending on the quality of the casting this joint may or may not be obvious. For rectangular objects, it's best to put the parting line right at the corners rather than in the middle of a face. Should the mold be slightly out of alignment when the pour is made, any slight slip will be obvious; while if the line comes at the corner where there is a natural demarcation, the error will be ignored. For irregular or round objects look for a natural seam or ridge to place the parting line. If there is no way to disguise the line, then place it in a location where any irregularities resulting from casting errors may be easily filed away on the finished casting.

Single-faced molds do not have a parting line and are frequently used for buildings that are made in repeating patterns. Of course, these castings only have a flat back with no interior details. Good pattern design here will save much time in the final assembly of the building. The factory-type wall in Fig. 10-11 is made from repeating modules from the same two patterns. Each

Fig. 10-14. Even the best modular patterns are not perfect, as this problem with a corner shows. We've simply run out of pilasters, needing two at the corner. A reject casting was salvaged, the plaster broken out and used to finish the corner. Being so easy to carve and file, the plaster casting easily fits in place.

window and one of the columns (pilasters) is a single casting. A groove and notch was cast into each piece so the joint was made behind the pilaster and is almost invisible (Fig. 10-12). The brick cornice at the top was cast as a separate section and made about 4 scale feet wider than the lower casting to eliminate a seam directly above the pilaster. Your eye would follow the straight line of the pilaster up and immediately notice the seam. By moving it over a few inches, the joint is less obvious. Can you find the joints?

It is very difficult to join bricks along a straight line; rather, the pattern should be stepped along the bricks. To my chagrin, I used a straight line in this model and in some places had great difficulty camouflaging the joints. In one case it was so bad I had to invent the drain pipe at the right of the photo which simply covers a joint in the cornice. For wooden structures, place the parting line along a board, edge of a wall or along the edge of a window or door. Take advantage of any natural line or junction to hide a section of the parting line. In later models, I've taken to casting the pilasters as a separate piece, then just gluing these over the joints in the basic structure.

Modular castings can be used for large, complex structures that could not be made in one pour. The octagonal chimney in Fig. 10-13 was actually made in eight sections (I cast about 14 to get 8), then joined together to make the finished stack. The cap is a separate cardstock fabrication. Although more complex than a beginner's project, the principles used to make the finished model are the same.

Save your substandard castings for salvage parts. The corners of the boilerhouse (Fig. 10-14) all required extra pilasters and some plaster filling salvaged from other pieces.

Remember to make all your patterns completely solid and well sealed to their base. The casting rubber will creep into every open space, including the interiors of patterns, completely locking the mold to the pattern. A little glue, putty, or modeling clay can be used to fill holes and imperfections in the pattern.

Take plenty of time in planning your pattern. Only one is needed to make all your copies. I usually take a large number of pictures of the prototype and spend a few evenings studying the shape and form looking, for parting line location, thinking about how the finished castings will be assembled and about how the building may be compressed without losing its flavor. A few hours at the beginning can save you dozens in the end.

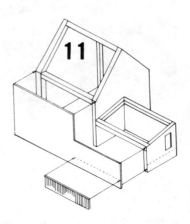

The Molding Process

Once a good pattern, properly designed, has been prepared, the working mold and finished casting may be made. There are two types of molding rubbers commonly used by the modeler—latex and RTV or silicone. I've used both, but find the RTV to be more versatile.

Latex rubbers are a water suspension of various hydrocarbon based polymer materials that form a flexible solid when dry. Because of the water, they must be kept from freezing and applied in thin layers to allow the water to escape. If the layers are added too quickly, the water will not leave the inner layers, leaving a mushy mold that never dries even with heating.

RTV OR SILICONE MOLDS

The RTV (room temperature vulcanizing) or silicone rubbers are normally two-part hydrocarbon based materials that must be mixed in a definite proportion, then allowed to cure or react over several hours—usually overnight. These materials do not need exposure to the air, so they may be covered or held in any type of container until solid. The rubbers are available from many manufacturers and suppliers and come in several grades. I use an RTV rubber called Castomold SR-P, which is a very light rubber designed for pouring with a low viscosity. Some form of box-like holder must be made to retain the molding rubber while it sets. The size of the box will determine the wall thickness of the mold. There are two differing views on how thick a mold should be. One group

Fig. 11-1. A thick RTV mold on the left produces wall castings for the boilerhouse. It is not very flexible, causing many castings to break, but requires no support and was easy to make.

feels that a thick mold is necessary to allow good support and prevent the weight of the plaster from pushing out the walls and distorting the shape of the casting. Thick molds, however, are not as flexible, are more likely to tear, trap more bubbles and, of course, use up more rubber which is expensive. They are however, much easier to make for the beginner (Fig. 11-1).

The second group states that wall thickness should be as thin as possible to make the mold very easy to remove, since a thin mold will be more flexible, release from the casting were easily, trap fewer bubbles, and use less rubber. A thin mold may in many cases require a second layer around it, usually of plaster, to act as a support and prevent the mold from distorting (Fig. 11-2, 11-3). This will primarily be necessary for long and deep molds; very small molds will not require support.

The mold box itself may be made of any material that can be glued to your base. I like to use scribed plastic sheet from Evergreen Scale Models because the uniform walls can quickly be made by scribing and breaking off the material along the precut grooves. The parts can be glued with regular plastic modeling glue and dry very quickly. If your pattern base is also plastic, the box goes together in minutes. The thin plastic may later be easily broken away when the mold is to be removed (Fig. 11-4). I always cover my molds with a piece of glass or plastic to be sure that the top of the mold box is completely flat. When solid and turned over, this surface will become the back of the mold. If the back is irregular or bumpy, the mold will distort and your finished casting will be warped. I have a very nice brick wall mold which will produce castings with a 3 foot warp in the wall. A little extra effort will prove very helpful in the end.

The first layer of rubber or mating surface is the most important part of your mold. Any bubbles, irregularities, or setting problems with the rubber will give you a less than perfect casting later on. The biggest problem you face will be bubbles. In mixing any of the of rubbers, air will be entrapped; should one of these bubbles attach at the mold face, it will leave a hole in the mold. Fortunately, this translates into a bump in the finished castings, so it can be cut or filed away, but too many of these imperfections will negate the advantage of casting many pieces.

Professionals eliminate the bubble problem by vacuum degassing the liquid rubber both before and after the pour. The mold is placed in a chamber where air pressure is lowered with a vacuum pump and the small bubbles in the mold expand and eventually burst. I built a simple vacuum pot (with the help of Dennis Storszak) from an old pressure cooker and salvage yard vacuum pump. This has worked well, but after the very thin pouring rubbers became available I just haven't used it. If you plan to do a great deal of very high quality casting, then a vacuum pot might be a good investment. If not, there are other ways of minimizing bubbles.

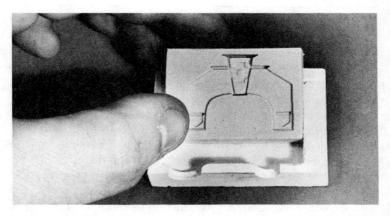

Fig. 11-2. A plaster box was cast to support the RTV mold for small window cornices. The larger the mold, the greater value such a support would have. Small round notches were made in the side of the plaster support to allow for removal of the mold.

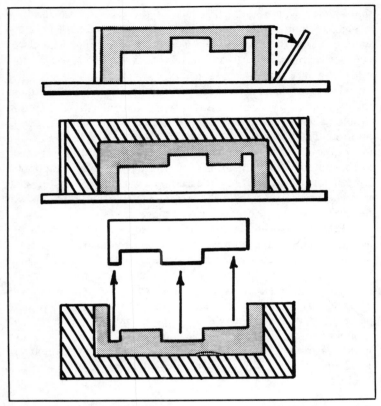

Fig. 11-3. Plaster mold supports (not to scale).

Since the mating surface is so important, make a special effort to eliminate bubbles here first. I mix the rubber according to manufacturers' directions, using a thinning agent if necessary. Fold rather than whip the two component parts together. Simple kitchen spoons can be used for measuring, while popsicle sticks make good mixing devices. Allow the rubber to stand for 5-10 minutes to allow bubbles to rise and break. Depending on the type of rubber you use and the amount of catalyst, pot life (time the material is fluid) should be about 30-60 minutes. Using an old brush or small stick, apply a thin layer of the rubber to your pattern. Bubbles can be seen and broken very easily. Work the rubber into all the edges, corners, and hard to fill places. Now pour the remainder of the rubber into the mold box in as thin a stream as possible. Being very fluid, the rubber will pour in a steady but almost hairlike stream which again encourages the breaking of air bubbles. I like to pour only in the lower portions of the mold and allow the rubber to flow, ooze and spread to the rest of the mold. By filling *upward*, there are no occasions where the rubber will fall over an edge and possibly trap an air bubble in the process. Slow and gentle are the key concepts. Overfill the mold just slightly, so when a piece of glass or plastic is placed over the top no air pockets will develop. Allow the mold to fully cure before opening. Molds can be made slightly more tear resistant by vulcanizing them; that is, heating at a modest temperature to further complete the polymerization process. I usually let my molds sit on a warm radiator or out in the hot summer sun for an afternoon to fully cure. Care should be taken about heating in the kitchen stove, as temperature controls are seldom accurate. Follow the directions from your rubber supplier.

Details for RTV molding are given in our casting projects.

LATEX MOLDS

Latex molds are best for making copies of *surfaces*, rather than objects that must have fixed dimensions. The most popular use is to reproduce the rough texture of rocks in scenery castings. If the mold warps or bends, that really is an asset since slightly different rock castings will be produced each time.

After finishing your pattern or selecting the surface to be copied, use a small old brush to paint on the first layer. You will find latex rubber much like paint, so a thin layer may be applied and all bubbles removed. Again the mating surface which will pick up all the detail is most important. Allow the first and every other layer to *totally* dry before applying more rubber. As the layers build up,

Fig. 11-4. Thin plastic makes an excellent choice for mold box material since it can easily be glued together, then broken away when not needed.

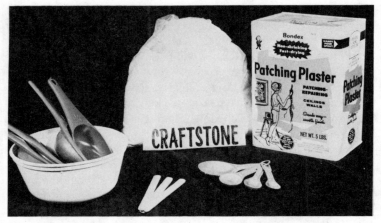

Fig. 11-5. The basic plaster casting materials include large kitchen scoop and plastic tubs for mixing plasters. Kitchen measuring spoons and popsicle sticks come in very handy for mixing. Ordinary hardware store plasters or very hard tooling plasters like Craftstone can be used for casting.

the mold will stiffen but still may easily tear. To increase tear strength, I dip pieces of ordinary gauze in the rubber and apply these with the fourth or fifth layer of rubber. Again allow for complete drying. As stiffeners, I sometimes embed pieces of strip wood or plastic in the final layers of rubber to give the mold additional support. Some modelers pour a plaster back over the finished latex mold to give good support for the mold. I have not been successful with that method but frankly have switched to the RTV rubbers where mold distortion was a problem. I cast the large brick chimney (in Chapter 10) in eight sections from a latex mold because of its size (over 20 actual inches) and the excessive cost of a complete RTV mold. There were many warped castings, but considering the low cost of plaster the inconvenience was worth it.

POURING YOUR CASTINGS

We have already discussed plaster's various forms in Chapter 9. Consider now the actual mixing and pouring techniques (Fig. 11-5). Bubbles again present the greatest problem and are more significant than in the molding process, because a bubble in the plaster will be a hole or a missing part in the finished castings. It seems the bubbles always turn up in the most conspicuous or important part of the casting. To minimize bubbles, I first put a few drops of soapy water (a little liquid dish detergent in a quart of water) into the deepest corners of the mold (Fig. 11-6). Pour the

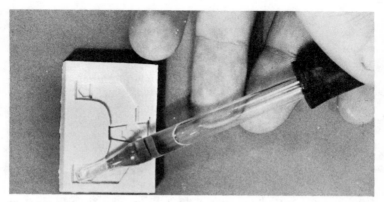

Fig. 11-6. A few drops of soapy water (liquid dish detergent in tap water) placed in the deeper parts of the mold will drive out bubbles: Use the same soapy water to mix with your plaster for easier spreading.

plaster in carefully, again trying not to splash or trap any bubbles. I use a thin mix of about equal parts water and plaster, which yields a liquid about the consistency of milk. Figure 11-7 shows two castings made in the same mold—one with a pre-wetting and one without.

The excess water will rise to the top of the mold, while the heavier plaster settles into all the deep corners and cranies. Allow the mold to sit for about 5 minutes, then cover the back with a sheet of glass or plastic, which will squeegee off the excess water and give your casting a flat back. The flat surface is useful for gluing the casting to other supports, such as a window cornice onto a wall. If all the castings have uneven and irregular thicknesses, joining them together can require a lot of unnecessary sanding and filing. If, however, you find your castings very weak and do not require a flat back, thickened plaster can be added to build up support. The

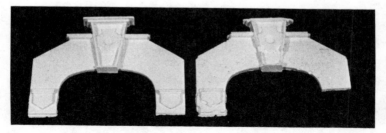

Fig. 11-7. Two finished castings show the effect of pre-wetting the mold. The casting on the right was poured in a dry mold. The corners did not fill, bubbles appear in several places, and part of the casting cracked away.

plaster should harden in no more than 20 minutes and the glass can be *slid*, not pulled off. Depending on delicacy, your casting may be removed at this point or left for several hours to dry further and build up strength.

For an especially large casting with many problem areas, I will drop into the fresh plaster several pieces of gauze—or better yet fiberglass screening—which act as reinforcing rods. Many of the boilerhouse castings cracked when removed from the mold, but because of the gauze embedded inside, did not break and could easily be glued back together from the reverse side.

Even with all precautions some bubbles may persist. The final solution is to partially fill the mold with plaster (just beyond the trouble spot) and plunge the mold with a small stick or hooked piece of wire. Drag it along the surface where the bubbles collect and knock them loose. Top off the mold with more plaster as needed. This will almost always give you some useable castings. If *everything* fails, then it's time to redesign your mold to allow for the release of the bubbles . . . change the shape, depth or parting lines.

I've never had a mold wear out, but I'm usually looking for only 5-10 good castings at the most.

As your experience builds, there will be other problems to be solved and new techniques explored, but that's part of the fun of model building. Let's go on now to some actual casting projects.

Building A Simple Highway Bridge

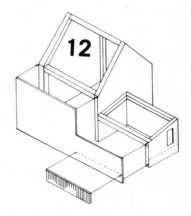

The railroads and the highways are not necessarily enemies. Goods delivered to central points by the railroads must be carried on to their ultimate destination by trucks and cars. In many cases both the rails *and* the highways share similar right of ways. Roads can undulate a little more, but basically tend to follow the same terrain. On the flat prairies of Illinois many of the older highways parallel the rails for miles on end, only sliding off the straight path to become a Main or State Street for the tiny little towns along the way.

During the 1930's and 1940's a multitude of small and large concrete bridges were built for the highways. Many contained small arched sections, some had flat sections and some even featured very fancy turned posts. The advent of the superhighways has eliminated many of these little cast masterpieces, but they still guard rural roads across the Midwest. Winter salt and errant drivers may have taken the sharp edge off many but still they stand.

For a casting project, the highway bridge makes an excellent first effort. I've picked a relatively simple style with few curves and odd sections. We'll be using a flat back or open-faced mold to make only one half of each side. This is the simplest type of mold to make for the beginner. Two of each casting can then be glued together to make the final side piece or a total of four to make the two sides. For a faster and more sophisticated approach a two-part mold would be better, but save that until you're more advanced. Study the scale drawings (Fig. 12-1) and prototype photographs (Figs.

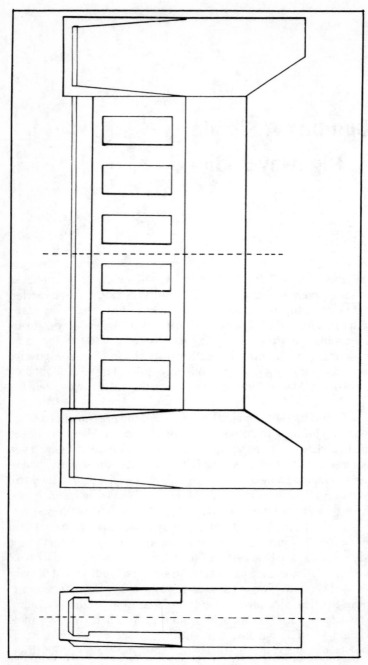

Fig. 12-1. Highway bridge (not to scale).

Fig. 12-2. The prototype for this little bridge is along Butterfield Road in Warrenville, Illinois.

12-2 through 12-4). How would you make the pattern? Remember not to include undercuts, and allow for easy removal.

I developed the pattern in the following way:

1. Select a piece of thick wood, composition board, or masonite as the base. Sand the surface very smooth.

2. Remember, we're casting only *one half* the side, so all the face dimensions will remain the same but all the thicknesses will be halved. The entire pattern will be made from sanded strip wood.

3. Glue a piece of 4 x 4 stock slightly longer than 8'3" to the base.

Fig. 12-3. The highway bridge makes a good first project for casting, since none of the dimensions are critical.

Fig. 12-4. If you would like a longer bridge, just add a few more posts, as required.

4. Cut 7 pieces of 4 x 4 x 1'9″ just slightly oversize. Clamp these together and with a file finish all to exactly 1'9″ or at least the same dimension very close to 1'9″ (Fig. 12-5).

5. Mark the center of the long 4 x 4 stock and, using a small square or triangel, glue the short 4 x 4 in place (Fig. 12-6). Using a piece of 2 x 9 scrap stock as a spacer, add the other short 4 x 4's (Fig. 12-7).

6. Glue a second 4 x 4 strip along the bottom. After it's dry, very carefully trim back the edges of the top and bottom 4 x 4 railings, square up with a file, and sand all the surfaces flat, tight and smooth (Fig. 12-8). The purpose of cutting the railings oversize and then trimming them back is to assure a perfectly spaced and very smooth concrete-like pattern.

7. Add a 6 x 6 railing at the top and a 9 x 18 base at the bottom. Again, true with files and smooth (Fig. 12-9).

Fig. 12-5. The small posts are clamped together, then filed down to exactly the same length. It's more important to have all the posts the same length rather than a specific length.

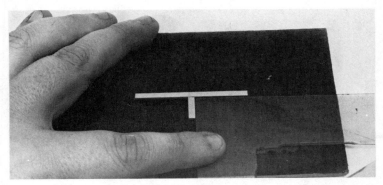

Fig. 12-6. Use a square or triangle to center and position the posts for gluing. The horizontal 4 x 4 post is tightly glued in place.

8. The two large side posts have a number of slanted surfaces. If the complex sanded pieces are too hard to make that's okay, just make them solid. Begin by measuring the large 2'9" side pieces according to the plans. These tip back approximately 3" at the top. Gang both posts together. Mark the spot the angle begins and with a file cut the tops back about 3". Be sure all the pieces have the same contour (Fig. 12-10).

9. To each of the side posts, center and glue on a piece of 3 x 12 ending exactly where the angled portion begins (Fig. 12-11). Sand this flush with the base of the post. This may sound a little complicated, but gives you the chance to make up a compound piece using only straight pieces of wood.

10. Glue the posts to the base and sand smooth again (Fig. 12-12).

11. Coat the entire pattern with a wood sealer and allow to completely dry.

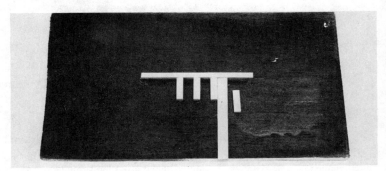

Fig. 12-7. A scrap spacer will assure that each post is uniformly spaced.

Fig. 12-8. Once the posts are glued to the base, the bottom rail may be glued in place and the edges accurately trimmed back.

12. Using scrap lumber or plastic, build up a dike around the pattern about 1/16″ deeper than the pattern part (Fig. 12-13).

13. The materials you'll need are in Fig 12-14. First coat the pattern with a commercial mold release or a silicone coating such as Scotchgard. Using simple kitchen spoons, mix the silicone rubber according to the manufacturer's directions. I used a good pouring rubber called Castolite SR-P from Castolite Company. A disposable paper cup is convenient. Mix carefully; don't whip air bubbles into the mix. Some modelers suggest using a brush to coat the pattern with a thin film of rubber. I've had good luck with just drizzling the rubber in as fine a stream as possible into a corner of the mold. Allow the rubber to creep and crawl at a very slow rate to

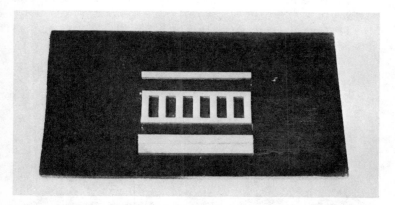

Fig. 12-9. Add the top railing and the bottom beam, which is actually two smaller pieces glued together. When this is sanded and finished it will appear as a solid piece of concrete.

Fig. 12-10. The side post must be cut back at the same angle for a recess of about 3".

all portions of the mold. Bubbles are your worst enemy, so be very careful and deliberate. When the mold is completely filled, cover with a piece of glass or plastic that has been sprayed with the release agent and allow the rubber to cure overnight. In the winter

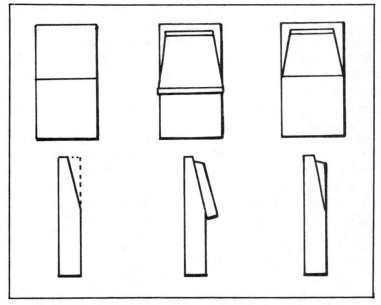

Fig. 12-11. Assembling the main posts (not to scale).

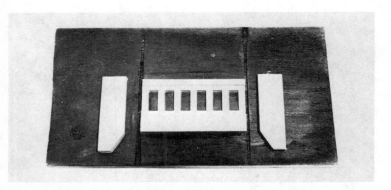

Fig. 12-12. The side posts are added to finish the pattern.

I place the mold on a warm radiator to vulcanize a little further, but that is probably not necessary. *Don't* touch the mold until fully set, as the partially set rubber can be a mess—believe me!

14. Finally—the moment of truth! Break away one of the edges of the mold dike and carefully peel back your mold (Fig. 12-15). You should have a perfect mold for one half of a bridge side.

15. For making the actual castings you will need plaster— either simple patching plaster or a harder stone-like Craftstone. Again the kitchen spoons are useful, along with a plastic tub from margarine or dessert topping (Fig. 12-16). I mix the plaster almost 1 to 1 with soapy water (a few drops of dish detergent in a quart of water is sufficient). The mix is rather thin—almost like milk, but flows very freely into the mold.

16. *Very important:* Wet the mold first with a few drops of soapy water, especially in the corners and deep crevices. This will cause the plaster to flow very readily into these hard-to-fill points and give you a much better casting. *Gently* pour the plaster into the deepest part of the mold, allowing it to rise and fill all the open spaces. Allow to set for a few minutes. During this time excess water will rise to the top of the mold. Place a piece of glass over the back of the mold to squeegee off the water and flatten the back of the casting. Since we will glue two of the pieces together to make the final side, they must be almost perfectly flat. Allow to set for about 20 minutes. Depending on your plaster and the weather conditions the plaster should set in that time.

Remove the glass and allow to air dry a little more. With the hard plasters you will be able to remove the casting now. The softer plasters may have to dry further.

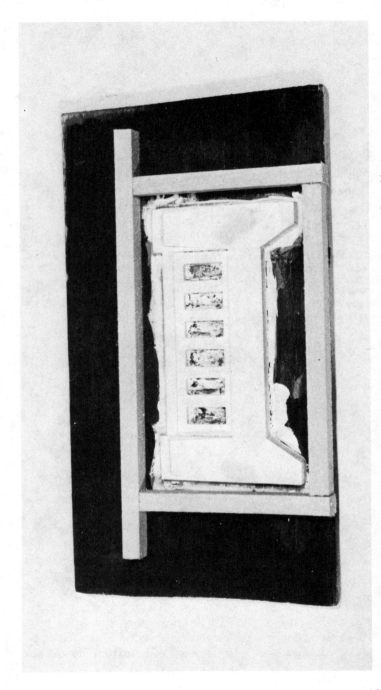

Fig. 12-13. In a scrapwood dike, the pattern has been coated with a wood sealer and is ready for the molding rubber.

Fig. 12-14. The basic molding materials include disposable paper cups, sticks, and bowls for mixing; an inexpensive set of kitchen measuring spoons for determining the portion of the rubber mixes; a fine pouring type rubber designed for modeling work (usually a two-part material); either a commercial mold release with old applicator brushes or a spray release such as Scotchgard; and glass or plastic to cover the mold.

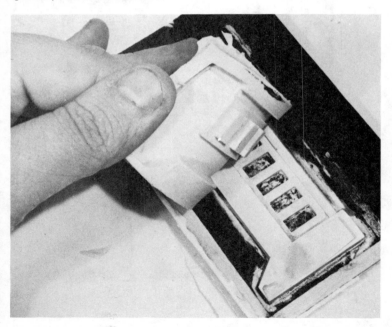

Fig. 12-15. After thoroughly curing, the finished mold may be pulled away from the pattern.

Fig. 12-16. The materials for plaster casting include again kitchen-type measuring spoons; either disposable or flexible containers for mixing; a few wood scraps or popsicle sticks; and either hardware store soft plaster or a hard plaster like Hydrocal or Craftstone.

17. *Carefully* pull and stretch the mold away from the part. Work around and around the part until it nearly pops free by itself. The finished casting should be a perfect copy of your pattern. If you waste a few while developing your technique, don't despair, since you only need four to make the entire bridge. If bubbles seem to be consistently trapping in one place, try this trick. While the plaster is still wet, take a piece of wire or a small stick and plunge the mold right in the offending area. This will usually dislodge any bubbles. Again, careful pouring and prewetting should minimize problems.

18. After the pieces have dried, glue them together in sets of two and file away any irregularities. Mine didn't match perfectly, but a little filing hid the problems. If you have a complete dud and

Fig. 12-17. Two of the castings are glued together to make each of the bridge sides; shown here temporarily set in an opening in the layout.

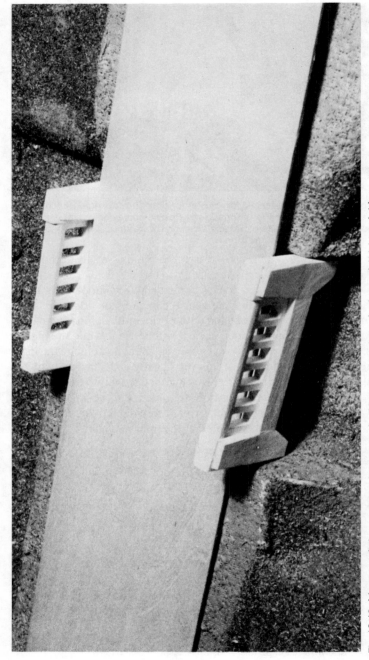

Fig. 12-18. A base made from a piece of sheetwood will form the foundation for the model highway bridge.

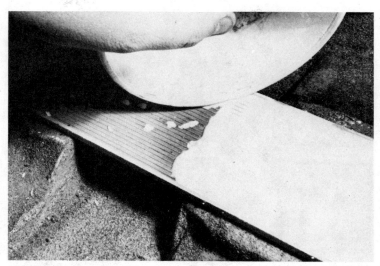

Fig. 12-19. With a small wood dike on each side, plaster is added to make the highway.

they won't match at all, that's okay too. Just make your bridge single-faced and position it on the layout so your visitors will see only the best side! A little theatrical liberty will never hurt.

Fig. 12-20. A few cuts are made in the plaster as freeze joints to help keep the concrete from cracking. Each bridge side may be simply glued to the highway base. The little abutments are just simple pieces of plaster sheet cut to shape to fit the dry creek bed.

Fig. 12-21. The finished model is a pleasing addition to any layout.

19. Figures 12-17 through 12-20 show the sequence of mounting the bridge. I used a sheet of wood as a base to pour a plaster concrete highway across the gap. The sides were simply glued to this base. A wipe of gray stain with a little mud coloring here and there finishes the model.

The finished bridge (Fig. 12-21) is a pleasing addition to any model layout.

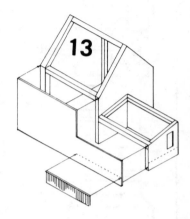

Building Cast
Brick Chimneys

13

Whatever era you model, chimneys are an important part of most structures. For heating, removing process gases and wastes, chimneys come in every conceivable size, shape, and character. Having worked for several years as an air pollution specialist, I have a personal affection for these towers into the sky. Driving or flying into a new town, my attention is usually drawn first to the chimneys and stacks. Of course, with the chimneys come industries and the *railroads* so there are redeeming factors.

Chimneys come in all sizes, from a simple vent pipe to the mammoth octagonal stack with my boilerhouse which was actually modeled at one-half its actual size since a full-scale model would not fit in my layout area. For our project I've chosen something in between—a modest chimney with some brick detail and a concrete base (Fig. 13-1). This type of chimney is found on many older homes and factories. By cutting apart several castings and then gluing the appropriate sections back together again, almost any size chimney may be created. Also, we'll be making a detailed pattern and using a two-part mold. This is somewhat difficult, but allows you to cast almost any three dimensional object.

Let's begin with the pattern construction.

1. We'll use the lamination technique here as we have in many of the previous projects. Begin by selecting a piece of wood stock about one scale foot square. Use basswood or pine, as balsa is too soft for this type of construction. Both the foundation and brickwork extensions will be made by laminating layers of wood

Fig. 13-1. Brick chimney (not to scale).

over your basic piece. Cut a section at least 6 actual inches longer than your pattern to allow for a convenient handle (Fig. 13-2).

2. With a sharp pencil and a small square, mark off lines about 3 or 4 scale inches apart on one face of the wood. For our chimney we need about 18-20 courses of brick. A larger chimney could be made just by adding more rows of brick.

3. Using the small square and a razor saw, cut grooves along each of the marked lines. Make these deep enough so the mark can be easily seen. This will probably be deeper and wider than the true scale mortar line, but a little character is necessary in order to be seen. Using the cut marks as a guide, turn the piece to one side and cut the adjacent grooves; then rotate the piece back and cut the opposite side. Avoid the temptation to just continue cutting the grooves all the way around the wood block. You'll find that small mistakes are inevitable and by working all the way around the wood block, those errors add together and your last cut just will not line

up with the first. Instead, by doing one side, then the other, and finally joining the side cuts at the back, the errors will still be there but they tend to cancel and the total error is less (Fig. 13-3). Do not use the square when cutting the last line. Just connect the side grooves.

4. Using a sharp knife, notch out the vertical mortar lines in the brick courses. Remember, these will alternate row after row and they should alternate around the chimney. Actually cut out a little notch rather than just make a cut. The groove should be about the same size and depth as the horizontal grooves. It might be convenient to use a pencil to mark a line near the edge of the wood so all the vertical cuts are in a straight line. Because the regular knife is so large, it's very difficult to notch one brick without cutting into the other courses. I took a #16 X-acto blade and, using a file, cut down the cutting edge until it was just slightly narrower than a single brick. With this modified knife a single brick can be cut easily.

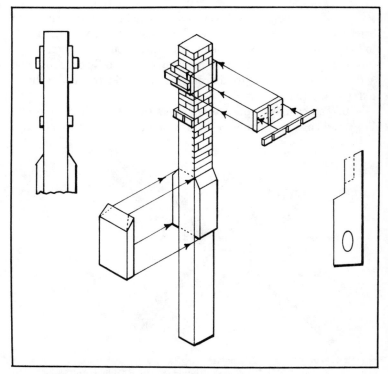

Fig. 13-2. Brick chimney construction (not to scale).

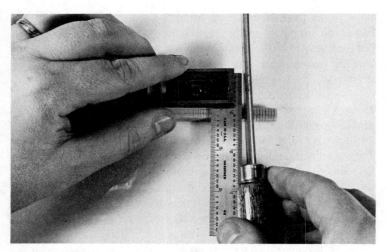

Fig. 13-3. Using a square, cut the brick grooves in the hardwood master for the chimney. *Do not* use balsa wood, as it will tear too easily.

5. The upper brick extension is actually three courses of brick. This is made by adding a 2″ extension all around the base, followed by a single course laminate. Each course is notched for the vertical grooves before the next row is added. Be sure to clamp and allow each piece to thoroughly dry. Add the lower brick extension in the same way.

6. The base is a concrete pier about 6″ wider than the brick. We could cut the chimney off at this point and glue it to a carved

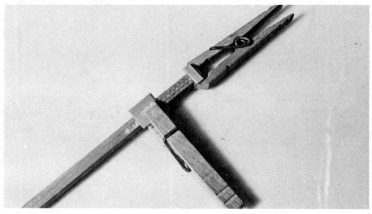

Fig. 13-4. Glue needs time to dry and form a strong bond. Here both the brick extension and the concrete foundation pieces are held in place with clothes pins while drying.

wood base. It would, however, be very difficult to glue the base and the upper chimney together in a true line. It's much easier to laminate 3″ pieces over the base on all sides and maintain a very straight line. Sand a bevel all along the top of a sheet of 3″ thick sheetwood. Cut sections about 10″ wider than the base and glue these to the chimney. Cut, sand, and file the tops, edges and corners of all the pieces that have been applied, including the brick extensions. Fill any holes with a putty like Squadron Green Putty (which is used by model airplane fans) that fills easily, drys quickly, and may be sanded and painted like wood. Excessive holes will allow the molding rubber to seep into the crevices and lock on to the pattern. Use your razor saw and knife to open any brick grooves that might have been filled accidentally (Fig. 13-4).

7. Carefully cut the pattern free from the handle and make sure the bottom is smooth and flat. We'll be pouring a mold in two parts around the pattern, so we need to actually hang the chimney in the air so one pour will go under it and one over it. Using sheetwood or

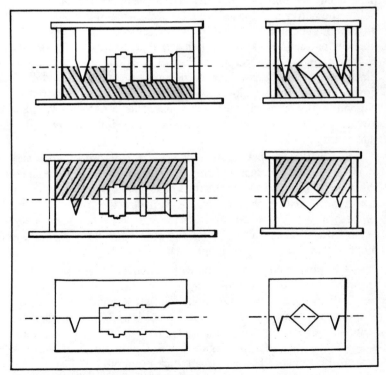

Fig. 13-5. Construction of two-part molds.

209

Fig. 13-6. The mold box has been prepared with the finished chimney master mounted on the side above the base so rubber will flow underneath it. Short sections of doweling will be used as alignment pins in the rubber.

plastic, cut sections for a box that will leave about 1/8″ above and below the pattern. Provide about 1/4-1/2″ around the pattern for alignment pins. Mark center lines along the end of your mold box, glue the pattern to it at the center and align so the corners of the chimney are on the center lines (Fig. 13-15). This positioning is to place the parting lines at the corners of the casting rather than down the middle of a side. Should the molds be slightly out of alignment, the error will not be obvious at the corners but will look awful if parted at the center of a face. Finish the box but *do not* glue it to a base.

8. Cut three short sections of 1/8″ or 1/4″ dowel stock and shape these in a pencil sharpener to a rough point. Cut these off so their length is about 80% of the thickness of box. The dimension is not critical, just so they penetrate well into the lower layer of rubber. Make six of these points. In place of dowel stock, ordinary pencils may be substituted. Glue the points in sets of three to a piece of scrap stock slightly longer than the box (Fig. 13-6).

9. Spray the pattern and box with a good mold release to allow the rubber to be removed later. I used 3M Scotchgard water repellant spray, but any commercial non-stick agent can be used. (Experiment first with some scrap material.) Mix according to manufacturer's directions sufficient molding rubber to approximately half fill the box. Once again, I used Castimold SR-P from the Castolite Company. Using a small stick or an old brush, coat the bottom of the pattern (up to the parting line) with a thin layer of

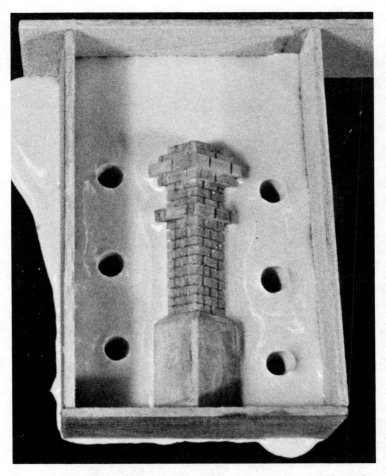

Fig. 13-7. After the first pour has hardened, the pins are removed. Notice that the rubber only comes up one half the thickness of the pattern.

rubber. Work the rubber into any brick grooves, under the brick extensions, and into any hard to reach place. Use only a thin layer so any trapped air pockets can be easily seen and removed. Now, with a *very* thin film of glue, attach the box to a base. Don't overdo the glue, as the box will be broken away when the rubber has set. Carefully pour the rubber into the mold box in as small a stream as possible; the finer the stream, the more air bubbles that will be broken. Air bubbles are your worst enemy so try to eliminate as many as possible.

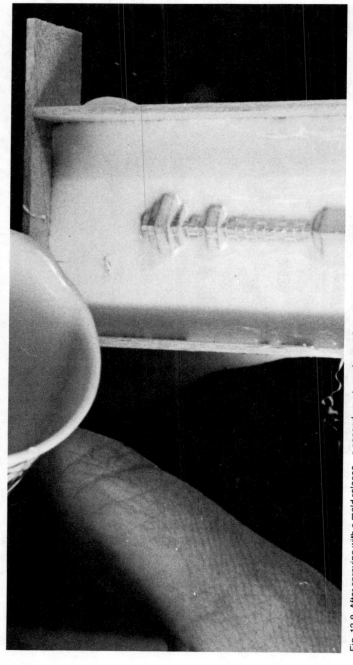

Fig. 13-8. After spraying with a mold release, a second pour is made over the pattern. First use an old brush or stick to coat the pattern with a very thin layer, breaking all the bubbles. Then finish with a fine stream pour to completely fill the box.

It may sound impossible to do all these things before the rubber sets, but if you've followed the manufacturer's directions, you should have 30-50 minutes of working time. Letting the rubber sit for 5-10 minutes before you pour will allow most of the bubbles to rise and break. Be sure, however, that you are using a *pouring* type rubber, which is much more fluid than many of the other RTV rubbers. Stop pouring when the rubber level is just barely below the parting line. Put the two sets of alignment pins in place alongside the pattern. If necessary, add *just* enough rubber to reach the parting line. Allow the rubber to cure for 12-24 hours (Fig. 13-7).

10. When the rubber has set, carefully remove the alignment pins without disturbing the pattern. Spray the exposed part of the pattern and the rubber face with the mold release agent. Be sure to coat the holes left from the pins. Mix another batch of rubber; coat the pattern, then fill the entire box with rubber. Use a small stick or piece of wood to plunge the alignment holes to be sure the rubber reaches all the way to the bottom. Cover this with a piece of glass sprayed with mold release. Add a weight and allow to set 12-24 hours. The glass is used to assure a very flat mold back. Allow the rubber to harden an additional 12-24 hours (Fig. 13-8).

11. Now for the moment of truth. Carefully break away the wooden box and ever so gently peel back the mold. It may be a bit soft at this point and likely to tear, so be very careful. If the rubber is caught in a hole in the pattern, reach in with a tooth pick or your tweezers and try to free it with as little tearing as possible. You should have a very serviceable mold. My alignment pins did not fully release but the mold is still usable. (Even authors have problems).

12. Reassemble the mold, using the rubber alignment pins to position the halves correctly. Two small boards or pieces of cardboard may be used to support the halves in a vice or similar clamp. *Don't* apply too much pressure, as the soft mold will distort and produce a very strange casting.

13. The castings may be made with either a hard plaster like Craftstone or ordinary plaster of paris. Mix a thin batch—just slightly more plaster than water—and slowly fill the mold, trying not to splash the plaster or entrap air. With a piece of wood or wire plunge into the wet plaster, especially at the corners and other areas where air might be trapped. Allow to dry, then carefully open the mold. With a little practice you should be able to turn out perfect copies of your original pattern. For troublesome spots, put

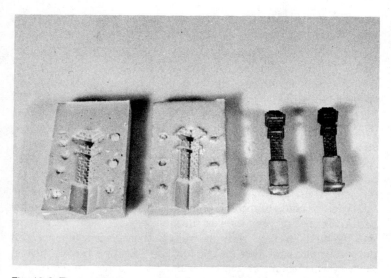

Fig. 13-9. The molding process includes from left to right: the two-part mold, a raw casting, a finished casting that has been washed with a gray stain and painted. See Chapter 8 (Trackworkers' Section House) for these chimneys in use.

a few drops of soapy water in the mold first and use slightly stiffer plaster.

Some molds may prove especially troublesome with pockets and corners that just refuse to fill. For a two part mold that is rather small yet deep, an alternate approach is to wet the halves of the mold with soapy water, then fill each side with slightly stiff plaster open face style. Quickly snap the two faces together and tip the mold so that no plaster flows out. Top off the open end with any plaster necessary. This can get a little messy, but is effective for difficult—to—fill molds.

As you can see, the molding process is an art that requires a little experimentation. I usually expect to have the first three or four castings fail while finding just the right combination of filling, poking and such. Even your failures should be saved though, since parts of castings may come in handy later. (Have *fun* experimenting. Remember, this is a *hobby!*)

14. After drying, the chimney may be finished in several ways. With a file and knife, clean up the castings as needed. I first drilled out an opening in the top, then finished this to a square hole. A drop of black paint or shoe polish will create a deep black interior of the chimney flue. I gave the casting a complete coat of gray wash to

tone down the white plaster color. If you are energetic, separate bricks may be colored different shades of red, black, yellow, and orange depending ont he sources of the bricks. A faster way is to take a wide brush, dip it in red paint for instance, then wipe off most of the color leaving a nearly dry brush. Scrub the surface of the casting with this brush, coloring only the tops of the bricks and *not* the mortar lines. When finished, wash the surface again with soem gray stain to dull the red color. Finally, with your finger rub on a little white chalk or plaster dust to again refill any mortar lines and blend the surface color together (Fig. 13-9).

Congratulations! You should now have some fine chimney castings.

You've come to the end of the text, but I hope that this is just the beginning of your interest in modeling and experimentation with scratchbuilding. Kits and ready-to-run equipment are certainly a valuable asset to the hobby and allow you to quickly develop a layout or mini rail empire. They are rather like the frozen food and delicatessen carry-out elements of a dinner. They make a fine basic foundation, but it always adds a nice personal touch when you top off the basics with a special homemade dessert. I expect that this book has somehow given you the chance to kindle an interest in building those special models just for your railroad. Nurture that spirit.

The ideas I have presented here are by no means everything any scratchbuilder will ever need to know. It is simply a start. Your skills are the sum total of the efforts you make—the mistakes and the successes. I trust you will build from this start and gain as much fun and satisfaction from model railroading as I do. Good luck!

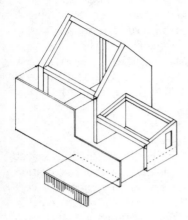

Glossary

ACC: Alphacyanoacrylate. Extremely fast-setting glue that cures upon exposure to water in the air. Best for bonding non-porous surfaces. Extreme caution should be used as ACC will bond skin or eyes instantly.

ABS Plastic: A polymeric material made of acrylonitrile-butadiene-styrene. Harder and more resistant than styrene.

airbrush: Small spray tool for fine-spray application of paints and stains with compressed air.

alignment pins: See Locators

back Saw: Fine toothed saw with reinforcing strap along top (back) of blade. Also called razor saw.

balsa: Lightest modeling wood; 7-10 lbs./ft.^{3} Easily crushed and broken.

baluster: One short vertical piece used to support a handrail or coping. Plural=balustrade; includes top and bottom rails.

basswood (American Linden): Light weight, close-grained wood used for many modeling projects. Harder than balsa; has a tendency to raise a fuzz when painted or stained.

bastard File: Grade of file according to coarseness: coarse, bastard, second, smooth.

board and batten siding: Vertical wooden planking with small wooden strips (battens) nailed over the seams between planks.

Bristol board: Heavy duty paper board with soft surface. Sold in thickness based on weight—10 lb., 20 lb.

216

butt joint: Wood joint where the end of one board is butted or glued directly to the second board.

caliper: Precision measuring tool for determining small dimensions between two jaws.

cardstock: General term for all laminated paper sheet material; usually cut with razor knife. Also see: Strathmore, Bristol Board, Museum Board.

casting: Making copies of an original by means of a mold and some free-flowing material such as plaster or resin plastics.

Craftstone: Casting plaster trade name of Castolite Co.; similar to tooling plaster. Very hard, impact-resistant when set.

catalyst: Chemical agent used to speed up a reaction. Frequently one part of two component mix for resins and casting rubbers.

chamfer: To bevel or flatten sharp edges and corners, usually at 45°.

compass knife: An instrument for drawing and cutting circles. Has two legs with adjustable screw between. One leg has a sharp point, the other accepts a pen, pencil or knife blade.

contact sheet: Unenlarged negatives printed directly on photo paper.

corner board: Trim on outside corner of wood frame building. Siding fits tight against corner boards.

cornice: Horizontal molding or trim which crowns or finishes a wall.

coursed rubble: Masonry wall made from random sized stones in crude rows (courses) with small stones filling the gaps. Farm foundations.

creosote: Oily liquid from coal tars used to waterproof wooden beams and piers. Simulated with black and gray paints.

cribbing: Framework of wood, concrete or metal beams filled with stones or earth to act as retaining wall or support for a structure.

cure: Process of allowing chemical reactions to proceed for rubbers or resins to solidify.

degas: Remove trapped air from a liquid, usually be lowering the pressure over the liquid.

dental plaster: Hard casting plaster used for molding.

die cast: Casting process where molten metal or other liquid is forced into a mold.

double hung window: Window with two sliding sashes that move vertically next to each other.

diorama: Small scene or portion of a scene usually modeled in great detail. Used by modelers lacking room for a complete layout.

draft: Slight angle on a master or casting to allow for easy removal.

Dremel tool: Trade name for motor tool. See Motor Tool.

dry brushing: Process of rubbing paint only on the surface of a material without any flowing of the paint. A brush is dipped in just a little paint, the excess wiped off, and the nearly "dry brush" is used to rub pigment on an object. Used for weathering.

elevation: 1) Drawing showing one side only of a structure. 2) Vertical distance above an established level or grade.

engineer's scale: A ruler, usually triangular in crossection, divided into several multiples of 10 divisions...10ths, 20ths, 50ths, 100ths, etc.

epoxy: Two-part (hardener and resin) thermosetting adhesive. Very resistant to chemical attack. Good for bonding nonporous materials such as plastic to metal.

escutcheon pins: Small pins or nails for ornamental fasteners. Originally used to attach keyhole plates.

flash: Small thin sections of casting material that has oozed out between mold sections.

fascia: Board nailed vertically to the end of roof rafters; sometimes used for gutter support.

gauge: The spacing between the railheads. Sometimes appears in common slang usage to denote scale; e.g. O Gauge. Standard gauge is 4 ft. 8 1/2 in. between rails. Narrow gauge is any track spacing less than standard. Common examples are 3 ft, 2 ft., and 1 meter gauges. Gauge and scale may be combined in a shorthand notation. On3 means O scale (1/4" = 1'0") with a 3'0" space between the rails. HOn2 1/2 means an HO scale model (3.5mm=1'0") but the rails are spaced 2'6" apart.

gauze: A thin, open-weave fabric; can be cloth or wire. Used for support in molds and castings.

grain: The direction and arrangement of fibers in wood, cardstock or stratified stone.

gypsum: Common chemical calcium sulfate used to make plaster of paris.

Hydrocal: Trade name of U.S. Gypsum Corporation for a very hard, dense plaster. Much stronger than plaster of Paris or patching plaster.

keystone: A wedge shape stone at the top of an arch which holds the other pieces in place.

lap joint: Wood joint where two boards are joined, each being cut to one half their normal thickness.

lintel: Structural element across the top of a window. Stone or concrete in stone structure. Does not show in modern buildings because of siding cover.

locators: Combination of male and female sites used to align and lock the halves of a mold together.

master: The original or pattern part. Copies are made based on the master. Jewelry and excellent brass castings are made from wax masters in the *lost wax* process.

MEK: See methyl ethyl ketone

methyl ethyl ketone: Volatile chemical solvent used to fuse plastic pieces together. Use only in well-ventilated areas, keep away from flames. Relatively slow evaporating.

methyl chloride: Volatile solvent used to soften and fuse plastics together. Use only with adequate ventilation and away from flames. Evaporates much more reaily than MEK.

modules: 1) Small sections of model railroads designed for portability. Can be joined with other modules to form operating layouts. 2) Repeating patterns or designs.

mold release: Non-stick agent applied to pattern or mold to prevent parts from adhering. Usually a Teflon or silicone type material. Absolutely essential for casting with epoxies, resins; less critical for plasters.

mortise and tenon joint: Wood joint where a hole is cut into one board and the second is cut down in a tooth fashion to slide into the hole.

motor tool: Hand held motor driven drill with exchangeable collects. Can be used with drills, saws, grinders, sanding discs and other cutting and milling tools.

muntin: Framing to hold panes of a window in place. Also called *glazing bar.*

museum board: Paper sheet used for modeling walls. Laminated material, but same color all the way through so edges need not be masked.

NBW: See nut, bolt and washer casting.

NMRA: National Model Railroad Association.

nut, bolt and washer Casting: Simulating the end of rod showing the protruding threaded rod with the usual washer and locking nut.

parting line: Demarcation or mark where two-part molds join. Can be made less obvious by judicious selection of mold position.

pattern: Original or master piece. Usually to be used to make a mold for casting.

pike: Short for turnpike or refers to a layout and general railroad scene.

pilaster: A pier or decorative column, not a supporting member, May have base, shaft and capital as part of the wall itself.

prototype: Original, full-scale practice or object. To measure a full-size building to be made into a model later is to measure the "prototype."

razor saw: Very fine tooth minature hand saw. A miniature type of backsaw with a ribbed reinforcement on the top to stiffen the saw.

resin: High molecular weight organic type chemical which will harden under the appropriate conditions. Generally not water soluble.

scale: A proportion in size. The most common scales are:

Scale		Proportion
O	1/4″=1 ft.	1:48
HO	3.5 mm=1 ft.	1:87.1
S	3/16″=1 ft.	1:64
TT	1/10″=1 ft.	1:120
N	1.9mm=1 ft.	1:160

scale lumber: Small pieces of wood cut to same exact scale proportions as commercial building material; e.g. O scale 2×4, 1×10; HO scale 2×12, 4×4.

scratchbuilding: Make a model or item from basic materials such as wood, paper and plastic without the use of a kit. Engineering drawings are optional and commercial castings such as windows and doors may be used.

scribe: To cut or scratch a mark or line. Scribed material has lines cut into it to resemble board joints.

selective compression: Reducing the overall size of a building, retaining the basic design elements.

silicone rubber: Synthetic two-part chemical material which polymerizes or reacts to form a flexible rubber-like solid.

sill: Horizontal piece directly below a window, usually angled downward slightly to remove the water.

single faced mold: One-sided mold with a detailes, flat back.

solder: Mixtures of metal which melt at varying temperatures with different degrees of hardness.

Solder	Melting Point	Strength
Silver Solder	high	high
Lead-Tin (40-60)	medium	medium
Cerro (Bismuth Solders)	low	low
	(about 212°F)	

Strathmore: Commercial name of high quality hard surface cardstock or paper material. Supplied in various thicknesses based on plies; 1-ply, 2-ply, 3-ply, etc. Cuts very cleanly with sharp razor or knife. Also see Bristol Board.

stripwood: General term for small pieces of wood cut to exact dimensions such as 1/32 × 1/16. Also includes scale lumber which are reproductions of actual lumber sizes in various scales; HO 2×4, 0 2 × 10. Lengths range from actual 12″ to 2′4″ depending on supplier.

styrene: A polymeric plastic material available in thin sheets that is easily cut by scoring and breaking along the score. Gluing may be done by pressing two pieces together and flow a small amount of the solvent MEK into the joint. The solvent actually dissolves a little of each surface then evaporates allowing the surface to fuse.

Super Glue: See ACC

symmetry: Correspondance of parts on opposite sides of a line, plane or point. A regularity of pattern.

undercut: A section or piece of a pattern or mold where liquid rubber or plaster must flow under a protrusion. Mold must be stretched or pulled to release casting when undercuts are present. A two-part mold can be used to relieve the problem.

vacuum chamber: Container used to lower the pressure over a molding rubber or casting materials to cause bubbles to expand and eventually burst.

vacuum pot: See Vacuum Chamber.

viscosity: Resistance to flow. Fluids with high viscosities (tars, molasses) flow slowly. Fluids with low viscosities (water, solvents, light oils) flow rapidly. Viscosity usually decreases with heating.

Vulcanize: To increase the strength and durability of a cured rubber or resin, usually by heating.

weathering: Process of painting, staining or coloring to show aging, use, or effects of weather on a model.

white glue: A polymer suspension in water. Sold under a variety of commercial names—Elmer's, Ambroid, etc. Some forms may be sanded. Others peel rather than sand.

X-acto: Trade name for extensive line of modeling knives and tools.

Zona Saw: Trade name for razor saw. See Razor Saw.

Selected Scratchbuilding Suppliers

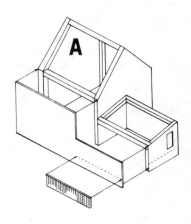

Brookstone Co.
127 Vose Farm Rd
Peterborough, NH 03458

*Fine craftsman type tools,
mostly woodworking.*

Castolite Co.
Box 391
Woodstock, IL 60098

*Complete line of casting
materials and supplies,
latex, rubber, RTV, plasters
in small quantities.*

Coronado Scale Models
1544 E. Cypress St.
Phoenix, AZ 85006

*Small parts, scratchbuilding
supplies especially for
narrow gauge models.*

Chooch Enterprises Inc
Box 3882
Glendale, CA 91201

Small detail parts - O and HO.

Craftsman Wood Service Co
2727 S. Mary St.
Chicago, IL 60608

*All types of specialty woods
(not in model sizes, however).*

also
1735 W. Cortland Ct.
Addison, IL 60101

Grandt Line Products
1040B Shary Ct.
Concord, CA 94518

Every kind of plastic component part possible; carried by most hobby shops.

Model Railroader Magazine
Kalmback Publishing Co.
1027 N 7th St.
Milwaukee, Wisc 53233

Major modeling magazine, covers all facets of hobby.

Narrow Gauge and Shortline Gazette
Box 26
Los Altos, CA 94022

excellent magazine for the scratchbuilder and narrow gauge fan.

National Model Railroad Association
Box 2186
Indianapolis, IN 46206

Monthly Bulletin, local, regional, and national meetings and groups. Well worth joining if locally active.

Northeastern Scale Models Inc.
Box 425
Methuen, MA 01844

Excellent scale lumber scripwood etc. Available at most hobby shops.

Period Graphics Supply Co.
29688 Franklin Rd.
Southfield, Mich 48034

Lettering, artwork for oldtime cars and buildings.

Railroad Model Craftsman Magazine
Box 700
Newton, NJ 07860

Major modeling magazine; covers all facets of hobby, especially scratchbuilding.

Wm. K. Walthers Inc
Terminal Hobby Shop
5601 W. Florist Ave.
Milwaukee, Wisc. 53218

Complete mail order hobby shop. All scratchbuilding supplies.

Index

Index

Edited by Steven H. Mesner